Crime Police and Correction

ALSO BY THE SAME AUTHOR

- Criminology and Penology
- Crime, Law and Police Science
- Public Relations at the Cutting Edge Level: Case-study Materials (Co-author)
- Bankers' Safety in Money Transactions
- Police and the Society (Co-author)
- Human Rights and the Police in India
- The Police and Delinquency in India
- Human Behaviour and Law Enforcement (Co-author)
- Indian Police and Miscarriage of Justice
- The Police, The Accused and Criminal Injustice
- Human Relations in Banking : How to get along better with people (Co-author)
- Police and Human Rights (edited)
- Polisum Pothujanangalum (Police and the People)
- The Police, The People and Criminal Justice
- The Police, The Court and Injustice
- Departmental Inquiries and Injustice
- Management Thoughts For Police Administration
- Road Users' Guide (Malayalam)
- Acquittals in Administration of Criminal Justice (Ph.D. Manuscript, Kerala University).

Crime Police and Correction

James Vadackumchery, Ph.D.

A.P.H. Publishing Corporation
5, Ansari Road, Darya Ganj, New Delhi-110 002

Published by :

S.B. Nangia
for **APH Publishing Corporation**
5, Ansari Road,
Darya Ganj
New Delhi - 110002
Tele. : 3274050

ISBN 81-7024-939-2

First Edition, 1998

Laser typeset by :
Computer Codes,
M-1, Virat Bhawan, Comml. Complex,
Mukerjee Nagar, Delhi-110009
Ph. : 7651700, 7653592

Printed at **:**
Efficient Offset Printers,
215, Shahzada Bagh Indl. Complex.
Phase-II, Delhi - 110 035
Tel. : 533736, 533762

TO

MARIAMMA, my mother.

She used to say :

"Crime is a crime – no matter who commits it"

CONTENTS

PREFACE

Crime, police and correction — they are inter-related. Managing the strategies for crime investigation, prevention of crime, dealing with criminals, correcting the crime-doers etc. need a lot of planning and understanding of the principles in management sciences. The police involve themselves in all these activities and most of them are said to possess little or no information of the managerial skills to implement their ideas in a meaningful manner. This book, it is hoped, will fill up the long-felt need to provide information to police officers on those aspects of police transactions.

Crime and correction are the two sides of one and the same coin. Several agencies come in between the crime and correction, but police are the most important agency who stand in between. They see human acts, evaluate them as criminal or not, set the criminal law into motion, arrest the suspects, interrogate them, investigate the offences, get the accused convicted and later have a surveillance on the inmates released from prisons. Necessarily therefore they should know everything about crimes and correction. Not only that, they must also learn scientifically the ways and means to deal with all sorts of crimes-traditional and modern. These management thoughts will be of immense utility for making an analysis of various types of crimes and different methods of correction. Surely, they will help better to deal with the problems with more confidence and self respect.

MANAGEMENT PRINCIPLES— CRIME, POLICE AND CORRECTION is a book that contains the latest research findings on the subjects fitted into Indian context. Investigating a crime as per law and by procedure established by law is indeed difficult, but to understand a criminal and then investigate the same is more difficult. To enable the police to investigate a crime requires a lot of understanding of the working of the human mind and the environments which made him to violate the law. The predisposing and the precipitating causes behind the commission of crimes necessitate a thorough appreciation of forces which worked within and outside the crime-doer. This book speaks of the many and various aspects of crime causation and correctional strategies. To be more specific, there should not be any scope for violating law for enforcing law.

Police have been investigating crimes ever since the inception of the service, but one wonders whether or not they were doing it in accordance to law, procedure and methods accepted by the Constitution of India and other statutes. The approach of the police hither to has been criticized to be faulty and one of the main reasons for the disapproval of police approaches has been the lack of knowledge in behavioural sciences and principles in management. Police are managers of law and order administration and they themselves were managing the affairs with folk-lore assumptions of human nature and behavioural dynamics. The police can no longer remain to be ignorant about the latest principles of management. It is primarily a man-oriented service.

Any criminal may be a product of his environments or a victim of his psychological ailments. The law may not take notice of these multiple factors behind the commission of crimes, but individuals entrusted to deal with crime and criminals can not afford to be ignorant of those factors. For, ultimately the laws are enforced for human happiness and social welfare. An instrument to ensure human happiness and guarantee social welfare can no longer be an instrument of human torture and misery. Every criminal should be corrected and every situation causing crimes in society should be identified for initiating remedial measures. The management principles laid down in this book is primarily meant to equip the police to understand the criminal and his environment better. Ultimately, it should lead to the establishment of a police service that satisfies the aspirations of the people in a democratic set-up.

Crimes are of different kinds and criminals are of different nature. Police have to deal with all kinds of crimes and different types of criminals. The principles in management vary or should vary depending upon the kind of crime and nature of criminals. The characteristics of each crime and criminal are of paramount importance in applying the principles of management. Many police officers who have no background in criminology, penology, victimology, correction, equal justice etc. should be introduced into the finer principles so that they enforce and execute the laws in a meaningful manner. This book, in that sense, will be of considerable use for all police functionaries.

Police service consists of personnel from the constables to the director general of police. Some are trained in the old school of police administration and management. Such people may still feel that the police is basically a force and therefore its methods of management will be through force, authority, show of authority or pseudo-authority. This approach will not and can not yield any good to anybody particularly when people everywhere accept human rights and Constitutional safeguards. Every criminal has his human rights and no police officer has any human rights more than what a crime-doer enjoys. If that is the reality, how can the police overlook the principles of management ? Many police organizations all over the world apply the principles of management in their day-to-day administration and a time has come that the Indian police can no longer close their eyes to these pleasant realities around them. Indian police is a part of the international police community and in that way the police in India have to work in tone with the international police thinking on the subject.

Colonial police and their management strategies are forgotten lessons in the Indian police history. Today, we have the democracy's police and the police in India celebrates its golden jubilee in 1997. Fifty years have gone by since democracy's police service has come to this great country of ours, yet people complain that the police do not show sufficient maturity in their thinking, attitude and approaches to the citizenry. Police Management or Management in police has never captured academic attention. No university in India offers such a subject. The administrators including those in police showed a Nelson's eye to this subject so much so that the police management or management in police as a science has become a neglected area. Indian police is Indian police and we need to develop our own literature on the management of the police service. This book may be helpful in that way.

Police officers are performing a number of functions—like law and order, V.I.P. security, crime investigation, prevention of crime, intelligence collection, petition, enquiry, etc. The principles of management differ very much depending upon the need and objectives of police functioning. Some officers have good aptitude to manage law and order situations while others have the capacity for crime investigation or V.I.P. security. As it is, everyone does almost all jobs so much so that they perform their tasks in the way they want them to be performed. There is the urgent need now to identify officers who have special aptitude for crime-work and to give them special training in the specific area of their interest. One can not make a mess of everything by allowing anybody to do things in anyway he likes. The management thoughts on crime, police and correction are intended for bettering those officers who show special interest and keen enthusiasm to manage crime investigation and to deal with criminals.

Police-criminal rapport-i.e., a mutual recognition—is what is not seen today. They entertain an attitude of mutual hostility and suspicion. Both distrust each other and this is primarily because there is lack of confidence. The criminal feels that the police do not understand him and the police feel that the criminal wants to fool them. Creation of a sense that justice will be done whatever may be the outcome is what is necessary today. For creating such a sense and confidence, it is essential to follow the finer principles in management and human relations. Professional police-criminal interaction is an area not very much researched into.

Police stop their work when a case has been sent up to court for trial. This is wrong. They should continue to work if they desire to develop co-operation among the various sub-systems operating in justice administration. The police, prosecutor, defence counsels, court, press, correctional institutions, after-care services and the public are sub-systems in justice administration and the police have to co-ordinate their work with all sub-systems so that there takes place a concerted effort to control crimes and criminal activities. Police alone can not do much without the help of others and their willing cooperation and support. This is a management principle. Commission of crime, investigation of crime, detection of criminal, prosecution of crime, adjudication of crime and correction of crime are various aspects in the process of the management of crime and every step or agency involved in the process is as important as the police in the society. The in-put into the process is doubtlessly a criminal and the out-put should be a reformed citizen.

For the preparation of this book, a lot of time was spent to study the crime-doers, the convicted inmates, the released inmates, the police strategies etc. Discussions were held with many experts in behavioural sciences, jurists, police officers and professionals in administration of justice. Researches were conducted to know various aspects of crime and criminals. The author thanks all those who helped him to make his work a success.

I thank my wife, Mary and daughters, Neethu and Neethie, for extending their total and full support to bring out this book.

The views and opinions expressed in this book are personal and based on research studies. They do not reflect the views of the Government of India, State Governments, Police or Home Departments.

The author thanks M/s A.P.H. Publishing Corporation for bringing out the book in a beautiful manner.

Thiruvananthapuram Crmgst Dr. James Vadackumchery

MANAGEMENT PRINCIPLE AND ITS NUMBER

ILLUSTRATIONS, GRAPHS AND INFORMATION

CHAPTER - I

CRIME AND CRIMINALS : IS CRIME NORMAL ?

1

If crime is violation of law, then everyone—everywhere and always—is a criminal. A man cannot live without violating laws regulating him and his behaviour. If he does not, then he is a saint and not a man. Accept the reality as it is and then try to control crimes. Eradication of crimes is an impossibility as human nature contains the ability to commit crimes and the capacity to control crimes. Police is not meant to wipe off crimes from human nature and society.

2

Traditional crimes mean crimes committed by people ever since their creation or origin. Such crimes—viz, murder, theft, rape etc.—have been in existence and they will continue to be in existence until the consumation of the world. Police may recognise this fact and let them make attempts to curb down the extent of crimes in society. The role is neither more nor less in this area of human transactions.

3

Modern crimes are the revised versions of the traditional crimes. The forces behind the commission of any types of crimes are the same. Man is basically bad and the "BADNESS" in him finds expression in the commission of new crimes—nothing more and nothing less.

4

The neonate commits objectionable acts and he/she is controlled by his/her mother. There are several people and agencies to control infants, children, adults and the old. Family,

PERCENTAGE CHANGE FOR DECADES 1951 TO 1991

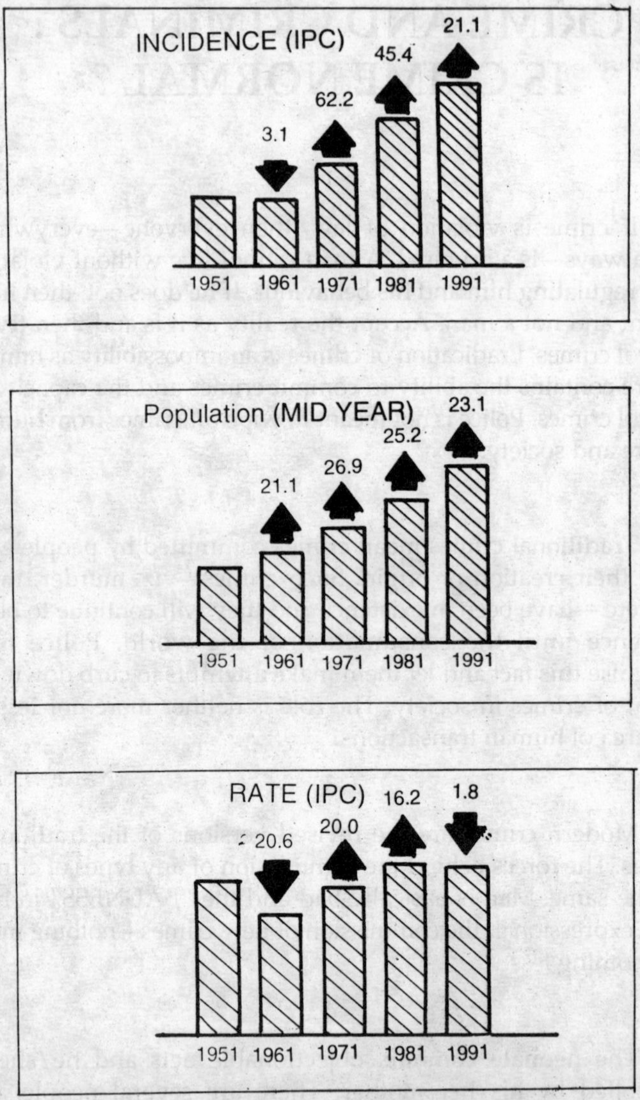

school, community, religious men, moralists and the media are but a few among them. Police too is an agency to control people and their behaviour. The police have an instructional role-like parents and teachers—to educate the people so that they desist from the commission of crimes and criminal acts.

5

'Organised Police' is of recent origin. Even before, there was policing in society. As people continue to commit crimes, society has to control the people. People want harmonious living and the society found that organised policing was a good idea. The same society finds that organised police is not necessary, it may abolish the police system it had created and it may think of a substitute. Remember that each society takes care of itself—either with or without an organised police force (service).

6

Can a man be a criminal always ?—everywhere ?—everytime ? No, he cannot, if at all he wants to be. A man is called "a man", for primarily, he is a man and then only he becomes a criminal. Policeman is a man, but at times, he too becomes a criminal.

7

Man is not a criminal, but there is a criminal in every man. And the policeman is not an exception to it.

8

Crime is essential for policeman—for, it is his bread, butter and source of livelihood. If there is no crime, policeman will not have any job to do.

9

Policemen, priests and preachers live and survive in society, because they know that people are there to commit crimes. If all people are saints, then many in society will starve. Many people make a living as there are people to violate laws and commit crimes.

10

When God created people, he created man and woman. God gave them some commands and the first thing man did after his creation was to violate the command of God—says the Holy Bible. Hence crime is as old as the humanity itself—but the policemen are of recent origin and development. Hence, criminal is said to be the father of policeman.

11

Why does a man commit crimes ? A police officer does not ask this question. He is interested to see only the "what" of a man's acts. If he has committed a crime, action is initiated. If the police were to know why does a man commit crimes, they may not take any action against many criminals.

12

Every human act has criminal contents. And the detection of the criminal contents depends upon how you look at it.

13

Crime is only a social reaction to human acts. Yesterday's crimes may be today's noble acts and today's noble acts may be tomorrow's criminal acts.

14

Beauty lies in the beholder's eyes. Likewise, interpretation of a human act as criminal or non-criminal depends very much upon how the viewer views it.

15

Sins, vices, immoral acts, evil-doings and crimes are related and show the tendency of people to violate laws—religious, moral, ethical, social and penal. Everyone is a criminal in someway or other.

16

Every crime has personal and social dimensions. Every crime has a victim and there is nothing like victimless crimes !

17

A man is free to commit crimes, but the freedom is to decide what he should or should not commit. There is no freedom as to "why" should be commit crimes.

18

Human mind has positive and negative energies. Expression of the negative energy is said to be a crime and in many crimes there will be both positive and negative energies.

19

Crime is a human act and very much a social fact. If it is so, every society needs crimes for its survival and progress.

20

Whenever a policeman gets angry with a crime-doer, it is the criminal in the policeman who acts and never it is by the policeman in the policeman.

21

A 'criminal after all' attitude is not the correct attitude to crime-doers. He is a 'man after all' and therefore he needs correction to adjust with the norms of the society.

22

There are multiplicity of factors which influence a person to behave in a particular way. If his behaviour is criminal in nature and content, it means that there are several causative factors to make him do the way he does. Try to have an insight into the etiological factors.

23

A criminal is born—no—he is made. But heredity and environment work together to make a person to become a criminal.

24

A crime can be committed only if there exist facilitating environments. Attempt to correct the environments before one tries to correct a crime-doer.

WHO IS A CRIMINAL ?

HE THAT MOCKS A CRIPPLE OUGHT TO BE WHOLE
(English Proverb)

"Let him who is without sin among you be the first to throw a stone at her"—HOLY BIBLE

"Early in the morning he came again to the temple; all the people came to him, and he sat down and taught them. The Scribes and the Pharisees brought a woman who had been caught in adultery, and placing her in the midst they said to him, "Teacher, this woman has been caught in the act of adultery. Now in the law of Moses commanded us to stone such. What do you say about her ? This they said to test him, that they might have some charge to bring against him. Jesus bent down and wrote with his finger on the ground. And as they continued to ask him, he stood up and said to them, "let him who is without sin among you be the first to throw a stone at her". And once more he bent down and wrote with his finger on the ground. But when they heard it, they went away, one by one, beginning with the eldest, and Jesus was left alone with the woman, standing before him. Jesus looked up and said to her, "Woman, where are they ? Has no one condemned you ?" She said, "No one, Lord." And Jesus said, "Neither do I condemn you; go and do not sin again".

25

All men commit crimes atleast once during his life. Attitude to commit crimes, the frequency in committing crimes and the persistence in continuing with the commission of crime are more important than the actual commission of crimes.

26

Crimes are committed by little children, adults and the old people. The forces which work in all of them are different only in degrees and not in kind.

27

Many people commit crimes, but only a few are detected. Still fewer are convicted. The convicted only become criminals in law. This does not mean that all others are not criminals.

28

Khaki collar crimes, white collar crimes, blue-collar crimes, no collar crimes—All are anti-social acts if the collar is removed. One finds differences in the attitude to crimes and they are made on the basis of the collar which crime-doers have.

29

'Conscious, sub-conscious and unconscious' are layers in human mind. Everybody has these layers and each layer expresses itself in human behaviours which may be sometimes criminal and at other times 'not criminal'. Understanding the working of the human mind is necessary to understand the crimes committed by people.

30

Policeman catches people who violate the laws and commit crimes. In doing so, the police too violate crimes. Who is then a bigger-criminal ?

31

If crimes are human acts, then crime-doers are human beings. If they are human beings, then they have human rights. Allow the criminals to enjoy their human rights which are their birth-rights.

32

"The last, the least and the lost"—This is the attitude which some people show towards the convicted to the correctional institutions. The approach is erroneous as they are the first and the best in many areas of human transactions.

33

Every criminal represents the society from where he comes. He gives suggestion for social improvement.

34

People who commit crimes express their ability to commit them. It is a warning to the society that the people should be more cautious and vigilant in life.

35

Pre-scientific theories on crime and crime-causation depended very much upon diabolical instigation and innate deprivity. As science progressed, the diabolical theories paved way for scientific interpretation of crimes and criminal behaviours. Still, there are people who believe in diabolical influence on people and people have recourse to exorcism and occult practices to curb down crimes. What a deplorable state of affairs !

36

Criminal motivations and facilitating environments were proposed to be the causes for crime and criminal behaviour. The approach is true and therefore one should look at the facilitating environments for fixing the criminal liability on crime-doers.

37

Exploitation of workers is said to be a cause for crime in industrial set-up. As a reaction to the exploitation, people organise themselves to fight against the exploitation. Who is more criminal here ?—the exploiter or the exploited ? Necessarily, both may be responsible and the crime can be reduced only if the forces causing exploitation and the forces fighting against the exploitation are identified before reaching a solution to put down crimes in such areas.

38

Lack of education is enumerated to be a cause of increasing crimes in society. Education and lack of it can decide the type of crimes and the way crimes are committed. For, a number of educated people commit crimes just like people who have no education commit crimes in society.

39

Inadequate recreational facilities are found to be a cause of crime by sociologists. Admittedly, it can cause crimes of certain categories, but, at the same time, adequate facilities or too much facilities for recreation can also make people to commit crimes. A number of crimes are committed during recreation and some people make use of recreational facilities to commit more crimes.

40

Defective glandular functioning in individuals makes them to show criminal behaviours. The crucial question here is the liability of people who suffer from such defective glandular functionings for the crimes they commit.

41

Police corruption is shown as a major cause for the increase of crimes in society. Is it true ? Corruption itself is a crime and therefore it means that crime causes crime which in turn causes further crimes and the process goes on indefinitely.

42

Neglect in religious training and commission of crimes are correlated—argue religious men. Criminologists may say that proper religious training and formation of conscience make people to feel guilty of the crime they commit. In that way, inculcation of religious values can curb down the commission of crimes.

43

Emotional instability and commission of crimes are correlated—say psychologists. Emotional instability can cause only crimes which have emotions as a major ingredient or components. It cannot cause other types of crimes which require more of intelligence and emotional maturity.

TRAFFIC UMBRELLA–A TAMASHA

A lunatic climbed over the TRAFFIC UMBRELLA and uttered loudly in public: "The commissioner of police is a fool."

The policeman who heard the utterances got annoyed and caught hold of him. The policeman understood that he was a lunatic.

YET, he was arrested and taken to the police station and a case was registered. While registering the case, there arose a doubt—i.e., under what section of law the F.I.R. should be recorded ?

The police officer who registered the case thought a moment and said: "Put two offences"—and they were—

ONE- for causing public nuisance

TWO- for leaking out an official secret in public.

44

"Criminals are not intelligent people"—early researches showed in this way. Now it is proved that only intelligent people can commit crime in an intelligent way. Many crimes of the modern world are intelligent ones and therefore they are committed by intelligent people and not by fools.

45

Fools commit crimes in a foolish way and they are caught by the police in an easy way.

46

Every scene of crime leaves traces of its criminal and an intelligent police officer can identify such traces. But it requires not only intelligence, but also efforts and persperation.

47

Frustration of the fundamental satisfaction drives makes people to commit crimes which come under the crimes against fundamental satisfaction drives—say psychologists. Surprisingly enough, people who have no frustrations to satisfy their fundamental drives too commit crimes which come under crimes against fundamental satisfaction drives.

48

Can broken homes cause crimes ?—ask the sociologists and their answer is always "yes" to the question. But criminologists may disagree with them saying that broken homes either directly or in itself do not and cannot cause crimes and criminal behaviour.

49

Psychoanalysts may claim that inadequate formation of superego in human mind may work as a cause of crime. Resultantly, such people may not have any guilt feelings if at all they commit crimes. Criminologists may further add that there is no individual who has adequate formation of his superego in every aspect of his dealings. It being so, everybody is vulnerable to the commission of crimes-nay-commit crimes.

50

An overeffect of "Id" complexes causes crimes and criminal behaviour—argue the school of psychoanalysis. "Id complexes" are many and they are in the "unconscious" layer of the human mind. Who is there in the world who has always only 'normal id effect' ? Everybody has "under-effect, normal-effect and over-effect' of id complexes depending upon many factors. Hence, everyone commits crime as a result of the over-effect of 'id complexes'.

51

"Normal behaviour" is a concept and abnormal behaviour is a reality. Likewise, crime is a reality and "no crime" is a concept.

52

Criminal is a man who exists and non-criminal is a concept and he does not exist in reality as a tangible being.

53

How can the crimes be classified ? Crime today is no more a crime tomorrow and crime today was not a crime yesterday. Crimes in one part of the world is no crime in another part. Some societies consider certain types of behaviour as virtues whereas some other societies treat them as heinous crimes. Why does this confusion exist ? Because, the crime is a changing concept—Is it true ?

54

There is nothing called criminal and non-criminal behaviour. What is criminal to one may be non-criminal to another. It is the individual's approach, attitude, reaction and interpretation which makes a behaviour criminal or non-criminal—Is it true ?

55

Criminal and non-criminal behaviour are human behaviour. If criminal behaviour is a human behaviour, then the criminals are entitled to get human treatment. Every criminal has human rights.

56

The fact that man commits crimes shows that only man will and can commit crimes. There are no crimes among the animals and insects.

57

Man may be able to live without food for some days, but he cannot live without criminal thoughts or words or actions for a few minutes—why then speak about days and weeks ?

58

Is there a person who is permanently a criminal ? No. Everybody is a criminal occasionally. Hence, what makes a man to commit crimes occasionally is more important than the person who commits crime occasionally.

59

'Born criminals'—this is a concept brought out by Cesare Lombroso. If criminals are 'born', then there is no meaning in making attempts to correct them. Correction of criminals is accepted and the strategy works well. If that is so, surely there is no "born criminals" in the world.

60

A criminal may be a learned person, for he knows more about how to commit a crime. The police try to learn how does a man commit the crime when they investigate a crime. Never underestimate the capacity and intelligence of crime-doers.

61

There was a time scientists thought that criminals were not intelligent people. Time has gone and now the scientists think that criminals are as intelligent as any other people in society and sometimes more intelligent than many other people in society.

62

Who are found in jails ? They are the convicted criminals. This means that there are many unconvicted criminals as well and they live in free society just like any other people live and survive.

A PRISONER'S DIARY

"I've spent 32 years here. Is that sufficient for what I did? I do not know the answer to that because I do not know how to measure punishment. I know that I have lost those near and dear to me while I was here. My father, my aunt who was a second mother to me, my brother. I know that I have forfeited any chance of amounting to anything. I have forfeited every chance of happiness. I've forfeited every chance of happiness. I've a chance for a family. Whether this is sufficient, I don't know"

(Quoted in the article 'Nathan Leopold after 32 years'.)

"May be you have asked yourself how can a man of even ordinary intelligence put up with this kind of life day in, day out, week after week, month after month, .year after year. You might wonder whence I draw sufficient courage to endure it. To begin with, these five words seem written in fire on the walls of my cell—"Nothing can be worth this"—this, the kind of life I am leading. No one knows what it is like to suffer from the intellectual atrophy, the pernicious mental scurvy that comes of long privations of all the things that make life real because even the analogy of thirst cannot possibly give you an inkling of what it is like to be tortured by the absence of everything that makes life worth living—a prisoner in prison cannot keep from being haunted by a vision of life as it used to be when it was real and lovely. At such times I pay with a sense of delicious overwhelming melancholy—my tribute to life as it once was."

(James V. Bennet, Director of the F.B.P)

63

Earlier, researchers used to go to prisons and penitentiaries to study the personality of criminals. Now, well informed research scholars do not go to penal institutions to learn more about crime-doers, for, they know that many criminals whose personality should be studied live outside the four walls of penal—security—institutions.

64

Conviction of a person alleged to have committed a crime to a jail means that he could not argue out his innocence well before a court of law. Studies show that there are innocent people as well in any prison population everywhere in the world. Really bad fate !

65

Are there any differences between the convicted in a jail and those who live in the society ? There are more similarities than differences between the two.

66

Every crime in society is a suggestion which says that there is something wrong somewhere.

67

Every crime is a matter of curiosity for people, for, the people are interested to know the who, why, what, when and how of the crimes. Hence, every crime arouses curiosity.

68

Behind every crime, there is a criminal and there are conditions inducing criminality in people. Conditions inducing criminality are more important than the criminal himself.

69

A criminal is never and can never be a criminal always and everytime.

70

A criminal is known by his act and a policeman by his attitude and reaction to crime and criminals.

OLD LIQUORS IN NEW BOTTLES

DIAGNOSTIC CRITERIA FOR ALCOHOL DEPENDENCE

1. Need for daily use of alcohol for adequate functioning
2. Inability to cut down or stop drinking
3. Repeated efforts to control or reduce excess drinking by "going on the wagon" (Periods of temporary abstinence)
4. Restricting drinking to certain times of the day
5. Binges (remaining intoxicated throughout the day for at least two days)
6. Occasional consumption of the fifth of the spirits (or its equivalent in wine or beer)
7. Amnesic periods for events occurring while intoxicated (blackouts) and continuation of drinking despite a serious physical disorder that the individual knows is exacerbated by alcohol use and drinking of non-beverage alcohol. (D.S.M.III)

71

A prison is a prison even if its bars are made of gold and silver. Anything done to improve the conditions in prisons can not make a convicted happy inside-always.

72

A fair-minded policeman is the joy of a detainee in police lock-ups.

73

An intelligent policeman learns a lot from a clever criminal in his custody.

74

A police service can be judged by the quality of service it renders to the criminals it handles.

75

A policeman is a diplomat if he can convince a criminal that he looks beautiful even in the commission of crimes.

76

Crimes are sometimes necessary for the progress of the society and for effecting changes in the existing penal laws.

77

A person in police custody is to be protected not from the crime he commits, but from the crimes committed on him.

78

An authoritarian police interrogator first loses his senses, and then gains the power of speach to question the suspect.

79

A corrupt police official is going to be richer next time and a criminal going to be caught next time.

80

An unfair police officer always finds another unfair police officer to admire him. Never employ third degree methods to elicit confessions from the suspects.

81

A policeman always dreams of success in investigation and a criminal too dreams of his success during and after the investigation. The success lies in winning the battle.

82

Some people commit crimes not because they want to commit crimes, but because they have no option other than committing the same. There is a victimological content in some kinds of crimes as the victim himself/herself may be a cause in commission of crimes.

83

A first offender is a first offender—not in the commission of crimes but in detecting him to be an offender in law. One's attitude to crimes to be taken in to account more than what crime he has committed before he is branded as a first offender or a recidivist.

84

Thief—is a label attached to a person who commits theft just like a person who is involved in teaching is labelled as a teacher. A thief can be a teacher just like a teacher can be a thief. A police officer is a police officer only when he does police work and he can be labelled as corrupt, unjust, cruel, dishonest, unfair, unlawful depending upon the nature of his activities during crime investigation.

85

An efficient police officer operates with his intelligence and not with his hand. Every criminal operates with his hand and not always with his intelligence. Hence, every scene of crime speaks loudly of its criminal. Conduct the inspection of a scene of crime meticulously, scientifically, methodically and intelligently.

86

A great police officer shows his greatness by the way he treats the less privileged, the handicapped, the poor and the needy.

87

A little common sense, a little consideration, a little sympathy, a little tolerance, a little goodwill and the police officer can know how comfortable he will be when he deals with a criminal while the latter is in police custody.

88

'Catch a thief to fetch a thief'—This is a wise saying. Accept the superiority of criminals in the area of his specialization.

89

'Crimes are acts or omissions which violate the criminal laws of a country'—Nothing more and nothing less.

90

Psychologists consider crimes as an abnormal act and therefore deal with them in a normal and desirable manner.

91

For the psychologists, a crime is an expression of a maladjusted personality and what is required is to help the maladjusted to make proper adjustment. A change in the personality of the criminal is what is required and not the destruction of the criminal's personality.

92

Crime is a phenomenon which attracts the criminals, victims, police officers, prosecutors, criminal court judges, press, media, forensic experts, defence lawyers, ordinary people in society, biologists, athropologists, clinical psychologists, psychiatrists, pathologists, neurologists, sociologists, psychiatric social workers, prison officials, probation-parole authorities, statisticians, religious men and so on. This shows how important is crime in the society !

93

Behavioural scientists consider criminals as people who are mentally defective, emotionally disturbed or maladjusted—more often victims of unfavourable circumstances or of lack of cultural and moral education. This may be true only with respect to

ALCOHOL ABUSE

DIAGNOSTIC CRITERIA FOR ALCOHOL ABUSE

1. Need for daily use of alcohol for adequate functioning
2. Inability to cut down or stop drinking
3. Repeated efforts to control or reduce excess drinking by "going on the wagon" (periods of temporary abstinence)
4. Restricting drinking to certain times of the day
5. Binges (remaining intoxicated throughout the day for at least two days)
6. Occasional consumption of a fifth of spirits (or its equivalent)
7. Amnestic periods for events occurring while intoxicated (blackouts)
8. Continuation of drinking despite a serious physical disorder that the individual knows is exacerbated by alcohol use
9. Drinking of non-beverage alcohol

Violence while intoxicated, absence from work, loss of job, legal difficulties etc. may be seen as impairment (D.S.M.III) certain category of criminals as we see today very intelligent, well adjusted and educated people among the criminals of all categories.

94

A policeman reveals his character more vividly when he deals with a criminal or portrays the character of another criminal.

95

A police officer who cannot ensure safety and security to a criminal in his custody will or can never give safety and security to people who live in his jurisdiction. People may desire to have more safety and security from such police officers more than from others in the area.

96

A crime may be one man's success and all men's wisdom.

97

People write books on crime and criminals. Sometimes they become the best sellers. This is an honour given to individual criminals who become successful in their activities. No doubt, there is an appreciation for what the criminals do although there may be a disapproval of what they have done.

98

In mythology, there was a king called "MAHABALI" in whose reign, there were no crimes of any description. Most unfortunately or fortunately, he could not rule the people longer. He was pushed down to a world under the earth. The moral is that a reign without crimes cannot exist.

99

Most of the crimes are quick acts based on long thinkings. Hence, there will be some traces left by the criminal at the scene of crime. Try to identify them.

100

A real criminal needs no character—no, it is not, for, there are many criminals who have better character than some of the law—enforcement officers !

101

A hard blow from a policeman to a suspect in custody is better than a false promise to him. Never be dishonest to a suspect whatever may be the success afterwards.

102

A starving suspect in a police lock-up has a natural right to demand food. Refusal to feed a detinue is an offence in people's law.

103

A starving suspect may confess any crimes and his involvement in the commission of crimes.

104

Infants are not born with an understanding of what is right and what is wrong. They do not have any idea about what the law expects of them unless they are made aware of it. Even in the ignorance of laws, they behave and at times, their behaviour may be against the laws. This means that there is something even in children and it makes them to commit crimes—knowingly or unknowingly.

105

Opportunities to violate laws—social, Cultural, penal, ethical etc.,—are found a hundred times a day and many people do violate them often. As usual, they are not detected and caught.

106

It is impossible to abide by all the laws enacted and implemented. Those who enact and implement them also know this secret.

107

What is a crime after all ? It is an act which some people dare to do at times! Criminals, in that sense, are courageous people !

108

God evidently does not intend people to commit crimes,

but he surely does intend people to fight against crimes. And how can the people fight against crimes ? The answer to this question decides whether or not the fight is by committing crimes against crimes or by other ways.

109

24 hours of uninterrupted contacts with a suspect in a police lock-up can make him really a good friend to the police provided that he is well understood. Treat him as a suspect and suspect only.

110

A police officer should be one who must know all about criminals and yet likes them. An officer in the correctional institution is one who knows all about criminals and still loves them.

111

Please understand that there are no hard-core criminals in the world. Every man is amenable to change as change is the only principle that does not change.

112

A police officer/correction officer shows his greatness by the way he treats the suspects/convicts entrusted to his custody.

113

Trust the suspects/convicts. 98 per cent of them are honest, decent and trustworthy.

114

Hating criminals means hating the job a policeman does, for, it is the criminal who ensures salary, food, position, good service entry, promotion and medal for meritorious services etc. for a policeman. Never hate him, but correct him.

115

Little children commit little crimes—think some of the police officers. Evidence is there to show that the children commit all sorts of crimes committed by adults and old people.

ENFORCEMENT CRIMINALITY

HE WHO IS ON THE ELEPHANT NEED NOT BE AFRAID OF DOGS

It is not what people commit that makes a crime. It is how the act is interpreted and the act is often so interpreted that it violates all the ingredients of the penal laws. On scrutiny, one may see that the offenders in law had the full knowledge about the ingradients of law so as to fit the act exactly in the definition given in the Statutes.

MISINTERPRETATION of a human act so as to make it an offence is an ENFORCEMENT CRIME and surely the people in authority can do so with some immunity as they belong to a privileged community when compared with those who are accused of having committed crimes.

ENFORCEMENT OFFICERS need not be afraid of the victims of their otherwise 'LEGAL' actions

116

There was a time when people thought that women usually do not commit crimes. When the dogs came to the scene of crime and started identifying criminals by taking scent of the perspiration, they could bring out several women who were culprits. Ever since, women are considered to be as good or as bad as men in committing crimes.

117

People commit crimes more against men than against women and the people who commit crimes are more men than women.

118

The crimes committed against women are found to be on the increase and the role played by women to become victims of crime is also found to be more positive than what it was earlier.

119

Victim-precipitation and victim-participation are two kinds of the role played by women in many of the crimes of sex-abuse on women.

120

Inciting, provoking, inviting, conniving, prompting etc. from the victims of crime often make the criminal to commit crimes. There is always a victim-victimizer relationship in many crimes committed now.

121

There is no single or simple cause for the commission of any crimes. There is surely a multiplicity of factors and therefore a multiple - causation approach to crime and criminal behaviour may explain the etiology of crime better than a single factor approach.

122

Nothing is an offence if it is done by a child under seven years of age—says the Penal Code. This means that the act is an offence, but there is legal immunity for the child from being proceeded against.

CHILDREN WITH ATTENTION DEFICIT DISORDER

(with hyperactivity)

CHILDREN WITH THIS DISORDER–

1. Runs or climbs on things excessively
2. Has difficulty sitting still or fidgets excessively
3. Has difficulty staying seated
4. Is always 'on the go' or acts asif 'driven by a motor'

CHILDREN WITH THIS DISORDER MAY SHOW-

- Obstinancy
- Stubbornness
- Bullying
- Temper out bursts
- Lack of response to discipline

(D.S.M.III)

123

When poor people commit crimes, everybody including the police may say that poverty is the cause of crime. Poor people commit crimes not only because of poverty, but because of several factors which make the rich and affluent to commit crimes.

124

The rich and the affluent commit property offences and they do so because of their richness and affluence ? The factors which make the rich to commit crimes can also be the factors which make the poor people to commit crimes.

125

If a person suffering from a mania commits crimes, he may have no moral liability for his act but he has the legal liability. He is considered as morally insane and legally sane when he commits crimes.

126

At the time when the crime is committed, is the crime-doer aware about the nature of the act ? - or - what he is doing is contrary to law ? If he is not, he is considered as legally insane and therefore, there is no legal liability for him for the act he does.

127

A person who suffers from phobia—or—phobic reactions–enjoys legal immunity for the act he does. He is considered as legally insane.

128

What is the relationship between heredity and crime ? There is no relationship—say research studies. Studies conducted on identical twins established this. Like physical inheritance, there are psychological and social inheritance for human beings.

129

Family studies to know the relationship between heredity and criminality proved that there was no relationship between the two. Never call a person to be a hereditary criminal.

130

Personality traits will not make a person to become a criminal, but they may decide how he performs as a criminal incase he commits crimes. There is nothing called "criminal personality".

131

Social structure--economic, political, social, religious etc—makes many to violate laws to have a change in the social structure. In that way, crimes become natural, necessary and inevitable for effecting changes in the society.

132

Crime is a process and it will go in different ways so long as man lives on this earth.

133

Some people commit crimes not because they want to commit them, but because they have no option other than committing the same. The compelling factors are more important than the act itself.

134

If all the crimes committed by people are reported to police, then the strength of police must be ten times more than what it is today. Some official estimates of crime show that not even 10 per cent of the crimes committed by people are known to police.

135

All crimes committed by people are not reported to police, all crimes reported to police are not registered; all crimes registered by police are not investigated; all crimes investigated by police are not charge-sheeted; and all crimes charge-sheeted by police are not convicted. Convicted crimes are just the top of an ice-berg.

136

If F.I.Rs are prepared for all the crimes committed in police stations, perhaps, the maximum number of F.I.Rs should be recorded from police stations—said a jurist once. Though the statement cannot hold valid in toto, behind this exaggeration, there is perhaps a lot of truth-observed a criminologist.

137

Punishment is the infliction of pain—physical, mental or both--inflicted on a crime-doer. When and how is the pain inflicted on the crime-doer and how long does it continue ? These are two issues which can be answered in a meaningful manner by the crime-doer himself.

138

The ability of a criminal is decided by the way he commits crime and the ability of the police is decided by the way a crime is detected. The detection rate is deplorably low means that criminals have better ability than the detectives ?

139

Crime is an alternative that is seized upon because there is no legitimate channels for social mobility—say the naxalites who commit crimes as they see that the legitimate channels to reach their goal are blocked by political corruption, bureaucratic nepotism and police lethargy. Is this view correct ?

140

Traditional crimes, political crimes, convictional crimes, organised crimes, white-collar crimes, professional crimes, personal crimes, economic crimes, property crimes, computer crimes, war-crimes, and what not ? How to define a crime is the greatest problem today.

141

Crime generates mixed reaction in the society. Some favour the crimes while others do not. Some tolerate them while others do not. What exactly is crime ?— No one knows anything about it although many people speak a lot about crimes and criminal behaviours.

142

Criminals are as much a part of the society as teachers, policemen, businessmen and professionals. As the society provides conducive environments for the scholars and scientists

General Rules of Conduct

PREVENTION OF CRIMES

Ahimsa (Non-injury)
Ksama (Forebearance)
Indriyanigraha (Self control)
Daya (Compassion)
Dana (Charity)

Sauca (Purity)
Satya (Truth)
Tapas (Penance)
Jnana (Wisdom)
(From PURANAS)

Forebearance
Forgiveness
Control over mind and heart
Non-stealing
Purity
Control over senses and intellect
Knowledge
Truth
Freedom from anger
(MANU)

Non-Injury
Truth
Purity
Good will
Forgiveness
Patience
From ARTHASASTRA OF KAUTILYA

WHAT IS HARMFUL TO ONESELF, ONE SHOULD NOT DO TO OTHERS. THIS IS THE QUINTESSENCE OF DHARMA (Mahabharata)

"Every person must have a standard by which he should judge his own attitudes and actions. An individual may be very careful not to commit a crime as per the laws of the Country, yet there may be full of sins inside. Sinful thoughts, feelings, wishes cause sinful acts. Clean your mind and then you can have a clean life "(PAUL JACOB (Chackappen), Vadackumchery)

PREVENTION OF CRIMES IS ALWAYS BETTER THAN CORRECTING A CRIMINAL FOR BETTER - MENT.

to work, so does the society offer facilitating environments for the criminals to work and flourish. The police ought to study the environments in which criminals operate before they plan strategies to control crimes in society.

143

Every society has a police service it deserves—say the policemen. Likewise, every society has a set of criminals it deserves.

144

Every criminal is a product of the community in which he lives and every community gives him the methods, ideals and goals.

145

Naxalites and terrorists may be treated as convictional criminals by the law and law-enforcement machinery. They may be , at the same time, considered as social reformers by a section of the society. History may say whether or not they were really criminals or social reformers.

146

William Bonger brought out—(1) criminal motivations and (2) stimulating situations through which the criminal motivations are expressed or executed. His concept about stimulating—facilitating—environmental conditions for committing crimes was recognised as good explanations to involve in crimes. Visa-rackets, false employment bureaus, fake shares and debentures, quack companies etc. are said to be the products of facilitating environments in the contemporary society.

147

Crime is normal in society and a society without crimes cannot exist because the fundamental conditions of social organisations logically imply crimes as well—said Emile Durkheim (1858-1917). Indian society has crimes which India can produce and so do all nations in the world. Crimes in India are normal to Indian society and they may not be normal in another society where the social conditions are different.

148

Crimes are not due to any imperfection in society or social life. They are there to perfect the society, social norms and social life.

149

Crime is normal, natural and inevitable in any society—this is what Durkheim says. According to him, crime is not pathological, rather, it is normal and inevitable. He says further. "Crime is a way through which the individuality expresses itself— the originality being expressed by a criminal.

150

Crime does a lot of social functionings. Crime suggests that the human society and the laws of the society are unsatisfactory to some individuals. As a consequence, the criminal uses his creative genius to break the laws of the society. Hence, for the evolution of society and its laws, crimes are desirable—says Durkheim.

151

A newborn child, when it becomes six months of age, develops to have teeth. When the child does not get sufficient breast-feed when it sucks or has difficulty to get the breast-feed, it reacts to the frustration causing situations by biting the nipple of the mother. This means that the child becomes aggressive to its frustration—causing situations. It also means that the child expresses its behaviour even when it does not have the teeth. It further shows that criminal behaviour is shown from the moment a child is born.

152

A new-born child bites the nipple of the mother when - ever it experiences problems which it has for the breast-feed. The mother feels it only on the sixth month when the child has developed its teeth. The moment she feels it, she reacts to the aggressive behaviour of the neonate by inflicting punishment—i.e., by denying the breast feed for sometime and there by creating an awareness in the child that it has done something which it should not. The mother also denies to the child its tactual pleasure which it enjoyed with the mother. All these are punishments and therefore the punishment starts from the moment a new born infant's violation of the laws is experienced by others in the society.

153

A mother punishes her child so that it may be corrected. The same principle is true whenever a person commits a crime in society. The society punishes him/her to correct the violator of law.

154

Though punishment to crime-doers is given from the moment a person is found to commit a crime, nobody still knows well how should the crime-doer be punished so that he is corrected and reformed.

155

Punishment is as old as crime and crime is as old as humanity. Yet, people do not know how and why should a crime-doer be punished.

156

Awarding of punishment is but just a process in social life. Just like marriage, education, treatment, religious observances, punishment is awarded to people who violate the laws. What can the society do otherwise ?

157

No country has got sufficient accommodation in jails to house all the criminals in the society. If jails are going to house all the criminals in the society, then the administration will have only jails. Jails are only symbols and they have only symbolic values as detention or punishment centres for detected or convicted crime-doers.

158

Many convicted people get themselves corrected even without going to jails. What is the use of prisons and penitentiaries if crime-doers can be corrected without undergoing incarceration.

A PRAYER BY THE CONVICTS

Oh, God
The Eternal Tribunal,
Who makes judgements on
human doings and misdoings

Oh God,
The Judge of judges,
who knows what is justice in
this world

Oh God,
The Mercy of mercies,
have mercy on me

Oh, God,
Pardon me for the ill-doings
I have committed and
bless me abundantly with
Your Grace.

Oh God,
Please give me the patience and
courage to live by abiding the rules
and thereby to reform myself.

Bless, Oh God,
the prison officials, inmates,
victims and all those who
work for the happiness and
well-being of the incarcerated.

IT IS NOT MY WILL

LET THE WILL OF GOD BE DONE.

159

Crime-doers who are convicted and who go to jails get opportunities to interact with other criminals who are better experts in the commission of crimes. Hence a novice in crime can perfect himself to commit crimes once he stays in prisons. Some of the jails are said to be training schools for people to involve themselves in the commission of crimes with better expertise and self-confidence.

160

A crime-doer is convicted to imprisonment after three or four years after his commission of crime. The fact that he did not involve himself in committing crimes during the period of investigation and trial in court is a sufficient guarantee that he can adjust himself in society without committing crimes. If that is the truth, why should he be incarcerated ? Is it for correction or for punishment ?

161

Jails were punitive in their nature and contents during their early periods. Later they became peno-correctional and now they are correctional in all aspects. Is this statement true in so far as imprisonment is considered to be a punishment for crime-doers?

162

The custodial aspects of prisons are given more importance than the correctional aspects. Can correction work well in custodial set-up ? If it can, then there is no meaning in recidivism in criminology.

163

How to correct the recidivists ? Can an individual be corrected and reformed without correcting the environments which influence him to commit crimes ? If not, more corrective steps should be initiated to correct the social melieu which makes the people to commit crimes more than correcting the crime-doer on an individualized basis.

164

When the society itself is criminal, is there any meaning in going after a criminal — or calling a person to be criminal ?

165

Punish the guilty-punish the guilty — This is a public cry. But many do not come forward to save the innocent or to aid the criminal justice system to punish the guilty. This is nothing but hypocricy of the first order.

166

There is a sub-culture of crime and criminal activities in all societies. The influence of this sub-culture is indeed very much. How does the sub-culture develop ? And how do the people become a part of this criminal sub-culture ? People who are interested to catch the criminal seem to ignore the sub-culture of crime and criminal activities. Why ?

167

There is cultural exchange and sub-cultural interchange. The media — especially the mini screens — is a source of the cultural and sub-cultural exchanges and interchanges. People who have criminal motivations are influenced by the media. They learn the methods to commit crimes and means to escape the police. How to remedy the situations ? How to counterattack the media influences ? How to control the formation of a criminal sub-culture by media invation ? All these are issues which need research and study now.

168

Material culture and non-material culture—and there is a conflict between the two. It results in the commission of crimes and this is called crimes owing to culture-conflicts. Old non-material culture and new material culture and how to reconcile them ?—how to compromise them ? Answers to these questions can suggest meaningful stategies to combat crimes and criminal activities in the present world order.

169

Human ecology has a positive role in the causation of crimes. Breakdown in the usual institutional methods of social control takes place in areas in which poor people live in urban setting. As a result, crime and delinquency flourish in such areas.

These are the observations made by a group of sociologists known as 'Chicago School' and they were interested in the influence of human ecology in the causation of crimes. In metros and other cities, crimes become a byproduct of the human ecology and what to do with them or how to go about them ? This is important in framing prevention-strategies and policy-decisions to combat crime and delinquency.

170

Death, fine, imprisonment, forfeiture of property and life-sentence were the different types of punishments awarded to people from 1860 under the Indian Penal Code. Crimes have been found to be on the increase and it means that crimes co-exist with punishment. If that is so, why should the people be punished ?

171

Punishment is an instrument for public justice and therefore it should be there in some form or other for the satisfaction of people. Punishment involves pain or suffering produced by design and justified by some value and if that is true, then it will continue to be there in society irrespective of its negative or positive impact for the control or prevention of crimes.

172

In ancient India, punishments were awarded with many purposes and they were—

1. to free the crime-doer from his sins
2. to preserve righteousness unhampered
3. to show honour to the righteous
4. to inflict pain on the unrighteous
5. to cure unrighteousness
6. to check evil
7. to make the kingdom safe
8. to protect the people
9. to restrain delinquency and finally
10. to make the king anger-free.

Could the punishments attain the objective ? Even when punishments were severely inflicted, crimes were found to be on the increase. Yet, people felt that punishments should be there, otherwise crimes would be more than what they would be if punishments were not there.

173

Punishments to the guilty and no punishments to the guilty—between the two, punishments to the crime-doer is found to be always better than no punishments to the crime-doer. Hence, continue please.......

174

Punishing the guilty—i.e., inflicting pain on the crime-doer-has some value and it is that value which forces the people to inflict pain on the guilty by way of punishment.

175

A crime-doer may have one thousand and one justifications for committing crimes. Likewise, the people in the society too have two thousand and two justifications to inflict punishments upon the crime-doers. For the larger interest of the society the crime-doers should undergo the penalty imposed upon them by the people in their corporate capacity.

176

No criminal has desisted himself from committing crimes for want of sufficient and justifiable reasons. Likewise no society has desisted itself from inflicting most cruel and inhuman punishment to its law-breakers for want of justifiable and sufficient reasons.

177

Society has resorted to all kinds of cruel, brutal, barbarous and inhuman corporal punishments to the crime-doers. Burning at the stakes, drawing and quartering, boiling, pulling the body apart and several other retributive methods were employed at one time or other in the penological development in the west. After all, what did the society achieve by inflicting such cruel and inhuman treatment to criminals ?— Nothing ?—Somethings?— Many things ?—or Everything ? Anyway, as years, decades, centuries passed by, the society decided to abolish all those corporal punishments saying that they were cruel, atrocious and inhuman. The decision of the society shows that the cruel and retributive justice did not ensure a crime-free society.

178

There was a time when people guilty of heresy or treason had their hands cut off and tongue torn out. The spies had their eyes plucked out. The society asks now : "Why were the people so cruel as they were in the past"? There is no answer to the question and no justification for the cruelty committed. Hence, the people feel regret for what their predecessors had done in the past.

179

Castrating the sex-oftenders or mutilating the sex organs, disfiguring of the face of the female partners etc. were the usual penalties inflicted in the west in the past. Such methods are not used now; yet some feminists demand that mutilation, castration etc. should be reintroduced to prevent sex-crimes now. They never speak about the purpose of such reintroduction or the rationale behind it. From the ignorance of knowledge, the mouth speaks out!

180

Branding—i.e., branding criminals with a letter indicating the type of crime committed by them was a form of punishment in the past. No society tolerates such branding now and yet in India, a few female criminals were branded by the police. 'Branding' is a human right violation and has no justifications in the present day society.

181

Enumerating the various types of cruel and inhuman treatment inflicted on crime-doers by society till now is a practical impossibility: Scold's bridle, brank, social disgrace, social humiliation, flogging, whipping, stocks and pillory etc. were a few among the many. All such corporal punishments have become a part of penological history as corporal punishments are fully and totally abolished now. Corporal punishments are human rights violations now.

VICTIMOLOGY

(1) Completely innocent victims—a child or a person who is unconscious.

(2) Victim with minor guilt—A woman—who agrees for abortion.

(3) Ignorant victims—One who does not know the consequences

(4) Voluntary victims—One who commits suicide

(5) Victim more guilty than the offender—One who provokes or induces other to commit crimes

(6) Most guilty victim—An aggressive victim who kills the attacker in self defence

(7) Stimulating or imaginary victim—A paranoid or a hysteric or a senile person

(Classification by MENDELSOHN)

(1) Female victim
(2) Young victim
(3) Old victim
(4) Mentally defective or mentally deranged victim
(5) Immigrant victim
(6) Minority victim
(7) Dull normals
(8) Depressed victims
(9) Acquisitive victim
(10) Wanton victim
(11) Lonesome and the heartbroken
(12) Tormentor
(13) Blocked and fighting

(Classification by HENTIG)

THE CRIMINAL-VICTIM RELATIONSHIP IS CALLED VICTIMOLOGY. It studies the victimhood, victimization, victimizer-victim relationship, victim compensation, victim's role in the causation of crime etc........

VICTIM - VICTIMIZER RELATIONSHIP

182

Capital punishment—should it be retained or abolished ? It is a matter of debate even now. The trend seems to be more towards abolishing it rather than retaining it.

183

What was that ?—Elephants were to trample over the offender to execute death penalty ? The most cruel criminal on earth might not resort to such atrocious act on human beings. Yet, the State in its corporate capacity did it in the name of administering criminal justice in ancient India. People who favoured death penalty also disfavoured this sort of execution by elephants. Can the society do anything on a crime-doer in the name of administering justice ? The society should be just, fair and decent even in its punishments.

184

Burning to death, pouring hot oil into the mouth and ears, inserting red-hot iron into the mouth, drowning after stones were tied to the neck, gorring by horns of the bulls, beating to death, beheading etc. were other methods of executing capital punishment. Were there not better and more decent methods to execute death penalty ? The society later found electrocution, gas chamber and hanging as better methods than beheading, gorring etc. In India hanging is resorted to. But the policy is to award death penalty only in the rarest of rare occasions. Should we still retain it ? The debate is going on.....

185

Debate over capital punishment is as old as death penalty and still people have not come to a consensus as to whether or not it should be stopped or continued. Human life ? or welfare of the society ?—This has been the question and the society thinks that social welfare is more important than individual's life in society.

186

Penologists may argue that punishment is for the correction and reformation of the crime-doer. In death penalty, the question does not arise as the crime-doer is annihilated. There is no one for reformation !

187

Capital punishment is not a punishment. It is a cold-blooded murder.

188

Crime-doers have been killed in many ways—by animals, by poison, by axe, by cross, by guns, by ropes, by suffocating, by drowing, by stoning, and by quartering, by being boiled to death, by burning alive, by beating to death, by precipitation from height, by gas, by electricity, by beheading etc. And what was the result ? Crimes have been on the increase and continue to be so irrespective of death penalty. Then, should we retain it ?

189

Capital punishment does not offend the provisions of the Constitution of India—said the Supreme Court in *Jagmohan Singh's* case. That is not the question here. Does the retention of capital punishment serve any useful purpose either in eliminating crimes or atleast in curtailing its extent ? If not, why should it be retained.

190

Who is punished more by capital punishment ?—the crime-doer ?, the victim of the offence ?, the dependents of the criminal ? Studies show that the criminal dies, the victims of the offence feel satisfied and the dependents of the crime-doer suffer and thus the punishment is more for the dependents of the punished. The society forgets everything in due course. Why should the penal method be continued ?

191

Capital punishment is usually awarded to manslaughter / murder of a cruel nature. Does the punishment deter the potential murderers from committing crimes ? The answer is "no", for any person who has determined to kill another does so whatever may be the consequences ? If that is so, is there any useful purpose being served by retaining death penalty ?

192

Is there any crime called death in custody. Obviously there

is no such crime; but if a person dies in custody as a result of torture, it is called "murder" and not custodial death. According to Amnesty International, custodial murders are on the increase. Beware of it!

193

No crime — including murder in any society will shoot up in an abnormal way. If it does so, it is temporary and the abnormal trend will come down to show a normal pattern. There will be only a gradual increase in crimes in any society.

194

Crimes in the Indian Penal Code - 1860 are indeed old. The new manifestations of the old crimes are seen and the problem is that one cannot fit the new patterns of crime in the old definitions as seen in the Code which was enacted about one and half a century back.

195

Police make use of only 17 sections of the Indian Penal Code often and another 17 sections sparingly. Also, they make use of some more sections once in a blue-moon and a few more in rarest of rare cases. Altogether they need to apply 91 sections of law from the Indian Penal Code which has over 500 sections with more than 300 penal sections. The old Code must be substituted.

196

The Indian Penal Code now in use in the Country is a pre-independent Code. The Independent India has never enacted its own Code even after 50 year's of freedom and democratic rule. The colonial Code still rules the democratic Indians. Rediculous indeed!

197

The Indian Penal Code enacted in 1860 and the Indian Evidence Act enacted in 1872 are two museum-piece - legislations. What a deplorable state of affairs !—that the modern crimes are evaluated by centuries old concepts about human nature and behavioural dynamics. The Evidence Act and its provisions are

THE INMATE

The inmate in a correctional institution is unhappy, because he is chained everywhere.

He envies the prison officials, because he thinks that they are happier.

But, if he knows how they live, surely he will pity them

THINK... THINK.... THINK ...Always

YESTERDAY IS A CANCELLED CHEQUE, TOMORROW IS A PROMISSORY NOTE, TODAY IS THE ONLY CASH YOU HAVE-SO SPEND IT WISELY (A Japanese Proverb)

ANY INMATE CAN WORK IN DIRT,
AND LEAD A CLEAN LIFE...Don' you ?

based even on folk-lore assumptions of human behaviour. How unfortunate it is to see that people are tried and punished only those Acts of antiquity.

198

A new Code of Criminal Procedure was enacted in 1973 and it was almost a replica of the old Code which was as antique as the Indian Penal Code and the Indian Evidence Act. God alone knows what advantage did the new Procedure Code bring out for improving the system of administration of justice in this great Country ?

199

Any number of crimes are reported, but detection is not much and conviction is still less. As a whole 7-8% of the total crimes reported to police and tried by the first courts end in convictions and the percentage is reduced to 2 - 3 when the judgements come out from the first court of appeal. If this is the true picture, why should there be this sort of futile exercise ? The real criminals escape punishments and it means miscarriage of justice.

200

Criminal justice system ?— Victim justice system ? — Equal Justice system ? — which is better ? A full and total justice can be ensured only under equal justice system — say the experts. If so, why cann't we abolish the criminal justice—victim justice systems ?

201

In criminal justice system, an individual accused defeats a mammoth police and prosecuting sub-systems. If individuals win over the police and the prosecuting sub-systems, there is something inherently defective in the system itself. The system needs a rehauling if the society needs proper administration of justice to the crime-doers and the victims of crime.

202

Every acquittal from a court of law means miscarriage of justice—either an innocent is falsely accused of or a real culprit manages to get an acquittal verdict. In both cases, there is miscarriage of justice. In some instances, there is more of sinning against the individual accused of than sinning by him. The system is defective and needs a total rehauling.

203

India follows an accusatorial model which is different from the inquisitorial model. Should we still eling to the accusatorial or shift to the inquisitorial ?

204

Everybody except the criminal may be guilty in certain crimes. Analysing the agencies and situations responsible for making a person to commit crimes is indeed a difficult process and to have an insight into such factors may reveal many things behind the commission of crimes.

CHAPTER - 2

CRIME AND PUNISHMENT: IS CRIME NATURAL ?

205

Look into the characteristics of the social melieu more than the characteristics of the individual criminal to understand crime and criminal behaviour.

206

Why don't all people exposed to the same social melieu become criminals ? Why do many people who are not exposed to the same social melieu commit same sort of crimes ? The psychology of the criminals may answer the questions better than the sociology of crime and criminals.

207

A person learns to commit crimes just like an engineer learns to do engineering work. It is through learning and association with people who do similar job. Hence, crime is also a learnt behaviour.

208

The process which results in systematic criminal behaviour is fundamentally the same as in the process which results in systematic lawful behaviour—said Edwin H. Sutherland. Association and learning are the two processes which make people to commit systematic criminal behaviour—Sutherland said further.

209

Criminal behaviour is learned. It is learned in interaction with other persons in a process of communication—says Differential Association Theory.

THIRD DEGREE

"Rudolph Sheeler, of Philadelphia, was arrested on suspicion in 1939 for killing a policeman three years earlier. Six of the city's policemen held the suspect incommunicado for forty days during which he was beaten, tortured and subjected to protracted questioning so that it resulted in a confession. The officers then trumped up a case against the man that resulted in his sentence to life imprisonment. After serving twelve years his case was investigated gratuitously by Professor Louis Schwartz of the law school of the University of Pennsylvania and found to have been gross miscarriage of justice. A new and speedy trial was arranged and Sheeler was freed. After excoriating the cruel police tactics, Judge Gordon stated that those involved "revealed themselves as unfit to be entrusted with police power". The six officers were suspended and efforts were made to compensate Sheeler for the great wrong that had been done to him" (From BARNES AND TEETERS)

....

....

"Clearly entrapment is a facet of a broader problem. Along with illegal search and seizures, wire tapping, false arrests, illegal detentions and the third degree, it is a type of lawless law enforcement. They all spring from common motivations. Each is a substitute for skillful and scientific investigation. Each is condoned by the sinister sophism that the end, when dealing with known criminals or the "criminal case", justifies the employment of illegal means."

(From BARNES AND TEETERS)

**THIRD DEGREE
METHODS ARE
THIRD RATE
METHODS**

210

Criminal behaviour is learned and the learning includes (a) techniques of committing crimes and (b) the specific direction of motives, drives, rationalization and attitudes—says Sutherland.

211

A person commits crime because he thinks that he can escape from being caught.

212

A crime is a crime, because the law says so. The law says so because, the society calls it to be so.

213

What is the relationship between low grade intelligence and criminality. There is, infact, no relationship between the two.

214

People having a low I.Q. may commit crimes as a consequence of their reduced power to judge the nature of the act or what they are doing is contrary to law. They do not know the impact of their acts to themselves and to others.

215

Prisons and penitentiaries contain the convicted who are not intelligent enough to escape law enforcement and a court trial.

216

The less intelligent people cannot commit crimes which require considerable planning and organization.

217

People having low I.Q. may become quarrelsome and are led by chance impulses and instincts.

218

People having low I.Q. cannot differentiate between the good from the bad. They cannot know the lawful act from the unlawful.

219

Criminals in general are not feeble-minded people. The mentally retarded cannot involve themselves in organised crimes, crime-syndicates or white collar crimes or crimes involving intelligence and planning.

220

People in general do not show any sympathy or consideration towards a person who is mentally retarded when he is caught for an instinctual crime he has committed. He is beaten and beaten severely. After all he is a mentally retarded and he deserves more sympathy and consideration than a person of intelligence.

221

When an insane person commits a crime—may be of violent nature—he is attacked very severely. What a strange psychology ? People have more sympathy towards the physically handicapped or socially handicapped than the mentally handicapped. Why ?

222

Psychological factors will not and can not ordinarily determine whether or not a person must become a criminal—rather, they decide on how he would function as a criminal incase he commits one.

223

Cruel people need not become criminals. But, if and when he becomes a criminal, he would commit the crime in a cruel way and so are the cases with people who are stupid, wise, prudent, aggressive etc.

224

Crime-proneness is universal, but crime-prone people need not necessarily commit crimes as they are checked and controlled by their conscience and other controlling environments.

225

People commit crimes because they are not adequately conditioned or they have not acquired an internalized conscience — says Eysenck.

226

A psychopath is described as a person who is free from neurosis, psychosis, or mental defectiveness — who knows the consequences of his behaviour but seems to have no inner feeling for what he verbalizes so rationally — who is habitually unable to adjust his social relations satisfactorily — who is not deterred by punishment — who lacks motivation — who expresses normal effective responses — who has poor judgement and who does not learn from experience — says Hervey Cleckley.

227

Psychopaths lack social emotions. They are 'lone wolves'.

228

Psychologists are also of the view that crime and delinquency cannot be accounted for as neurotic behaviour. They say that criminality cannot be viewed as a result of neurotic diseases, for, certain types of criminality are very skilled and directed properly e.g., professional crimes and crime-syndicates.

229

The mood and temper of the public with regard to the treatment of crime and criminals has been always an unfailing test of the civilization in any country — said Winston Churchil. Retribution, deterrence, reformation, expiation, incapaciation, protection of the society, correction of the criminal etc. were tried as objectives of punishment, yet, no one knows for certain as to how and why should a crime-doer be punished.

230

Retributive theory of criminal justice could create only law made cripples. In other words, one legged, one eyed, one handed, tongueless people could be increased by administering retributive criminal justice. Society protested against this inhuman and barbarous method and the result has been a shift from an utter unconcern to the criminal and his personality to a more positive approach of correcting him as a law-abiding citizen.

231

People in the society have still a retributive approach to

From

THE NATIONAL HUMAN RIGHTS COMMISSION

ANNUAL REPORT : 1995-1996

"During the course of the calendar year 1994, 65 deaths were reported in police custody and 34 in jail custody. In 1995, 105 such deaths were reported in police custody and 207 in jail custody. Between 1, January-31 March, 1996 a further 47 deaths were reported in police custody and 112 deaths in jail custody"

OBSERVATIONS OF NHRC

"A Magisterial enquiry revealed that Abdul Gafar Khan's death was caused by brutal beatings..... to multiple injuries which were antimortem ...." (Custodial Death in police in Goa)

".... the brutal murder in police custody of Deshraj by pouring kerosene on him was perhaps without parallel. It surpassed our imagination as to how, unless there be personal animosity, a police officer should think of putting the accused to death by pouring kerosene oil on him and lighting a match stick"... Rs 300000/- was given as compensation.

"..... Uma was indeed raped by the head constable.... the State Government sanctioned Rs. 100000/- as compensation to Uma"

Stripping of teenagers in police lock up...." The Government has sanctioned payment of compensation of Rs. 10000/- to each of the seven boys who were stripped and forced to spend two nights in the police lock-up".

".... The complainant alleged that the police personnel used filthy language and threw away some of his belongings...."

WHAT IS THIS ? AND AN ANSWER TO THE QUESTION GIVES THE EXTENT OF HUMAN RIGHTS VIOLATIONS IN POLICE SERVICE.

crime-doers. The people have a retributive rationable which is based on vindictivess towards the crime-doers. Experience has proved that the approach did not yield any individual happiness and social welfare.

232

The psychological impact of the retributive approach to crime-doers was found to be not favourable to correction and reformation of the offenders. Though in theory, the retributive approach was discarded, in police circles, it assumed various forms and shapes. Muscle power and third degree methods have been used not only to deter the people but also to show the retributive approach to the crime-doers. Human rights activists, commissions of inquiry, law commissions, press and media, police commissions and the people in general did not favour the retributive approach of police to the suspects in crime and crime-doers. There is a change in police attitude in these days and it is more towards correction and reformation.

233

Cruel punishments have an inevitable tendency to produce more cruelty among the law enforcement agencies. Thus jails became torture-centres and police lock-ups were turned to be places for roughing up criminals. The approach is disfavoured after the acceptance of human rights of the detainees in a meaningful manner.

234

Punishment can deter people and potential criminals. But, when the State has been vigorously punitive, the empirical studies showed that crimes were on the increase. Beyond a certain level of deterrence, punishments cease to have any deterrence value.

235

Law enforcement officers — particularly the police and jail officials — have been found to deal with criminals in a retributive spirit under the pretext of causing deterrence to potential criminals. Studies showed that deterrence for deterrence sake was not deterrent at all.

236

Experience has taught that it is certainty of punishment rather than the severity that deters criminals and potential criminals. Never be too deterrent to anybody including crime-doers.

237

Deterrence and retribution paved way for incapaciation in penological development. As a result, in 1704, the first jail was established in Rome to house the convicted criminals. Incapaciation was the aim in such constructions of prisons.

238

As time passed by, more of the prisons and penitentiaries were constructed in many parts of the world. The theory of incapaciation in security institutions was modified to include reformation of the convicted. Thus, the penal centres became peno-correctional.

239

Prisons, it was hoped, would give an atmosphere for the wrong-doers to have atonement on their sinful acts. But the hope was not fulfilled as the prisoners did not change much inspite of their long stay in the penitentiaries. Studies conducted proved further that like deterrence, incapaciation had essentially negative goals.

240

Short-term sentences to stay in prisons had no impact upon the crime-doers. All the prisoners incarceated come out of jails in due course without much changes in their attitude to crimes and outlook to a life of crime. Recidivists were found in plenty among those who came out of prisons.

241

Transportation to penal colonies was stopped as it was found to be a useless penal measure. Also, there were no places to be used as penal colonies. Transportation to penal colonies was not conducive for correction and reformation.

242

Too short or too long confinement in penal institutions was found to be not conducive for correction and reformation of offenders. A large number of criminals who are no threats to the public need not be sent to prison as imprisonment is found to have evil effects for the reformation of offenders.

243

Many prisons have no scientific methods for correcting the wrong-doers and almost all of them have no qualified personnel to do the job. As a result, some who go to jails become jail-birds.

244

Inmates in prisons have contacts and associations and they have very bad impacts on the incarcerated.

245

Should there be jails in the way they are today ? There are penologists who advocate that the penitentiary system should be abolished. But what is the alternative ?

246

Though correction and rehabilitation are accepted as the twin objectives of imprisonment, one finds that the correctional aspect is given only a secondary priority when compared to the custodial aspect. The guide-lines are still peno-correctional.

247

Imprisonment ensures protection of the society from the crime doers so long as they are in the jails. But, what about the protection once they are set free from the prisons and that too without effecting any change in their attitude and approach to crimes ?

248

Punishments may ensure social reconstruction. This may work in the long run in cases of social legislations. But, the philosophy may not hold good in case of traditional crimes like theft, rape, murder etc.

CRIME OF TORTURE

Any act of torture or other cruel, inhuman or degrading treatment or punishment is an offence to human dignity and shall be condemned as a denial of the purposes of the Charter of the United Nations and as a violation of human rights and fundamental freedoms proclaimed in the Universal Declaration of Human rights

DECLARATION ON THE PROTECTION OF ALL PERSONS FROM BEING SUBJECTED TO TORTURE AND OTHER CRUEL, INHUMAN OR DEGRADING TREATMENT OR PUNISHMENT

U.N. Convention Against Torture

"Surely one of the most insidious evils in this supposedly modern age is the continued practice of inflicting torture upon individual human beings. This Convention marks, therefore, an extremely important milestone in the continuing efforts of the United Nations to promote and ensure greater respect for human rights. The world community has thus outlawed once and for all the abominable practice of torture."

THE SECRETARY GENERAL OF THE UNITED NATIONS, CONVENTION AGAINST TORTURE AND OTHER CRUEL, INHUMAN OR DEGRADING TREATMENT OR PUNISHMENT

Human Rights Violations by Police

"THE POLICE ARE NOT TO VIOLATE HUMAN RIGHTS; RATHER THEY ARE LEGALLY BOUND TO PROTECT THEM. MOST UNFORTUNATELY, THE NEAR-TOTAL IGNORANCE OF POLICE PERSONNEL ABOUT THE NATURE, TYPES AND OBJECTIVES OF HUMAN RIGHTS IS BLAMED TO BE ONE OF THE MAIN REASONS FOR THEIR ADOPTING A DISMISSIVE ATTITUDE FOR THE LARGE SCALE ACCEPTANCE OF THE INHERENT, INALIENABLE AND FUNDAMENTAL RIGHTS OF MAN."

JAMES VADACKUMCHERY, CRIMINOLOGIST IN THE PREFACE TO THE BOOK 'HUMAN RIGHTS & THE POLICE IN INDIA'

Human Rights Violations are Crimes

249

A compromise between deterrence and reformation is considered to be the best objective of punishment. The deterrent-reformative approach has both preventive and curative effects. It doubtlessly deters potential criminals and cures the convicted offenders. Experience so far shows that punishment neither deters potential criminals in many instances nor cures the convicted who are recidivists. The objective is good but the methods to implement the objective have not been sufficiently matured.

250

Correction of offenders is a desirable objective. Criminal needs treatment and behaviour modifications. Experience shows that many convicted to the jails are first offenders or short-termers. As such, they do not require any special treatments which take long period. Further, many convicted to the prisons do not have any specific psychological problems which call for specialized treatment. Over and above, the prisons today do not have sufficient specialists to undertake special treatment programmes for the convicted.

251

Political crimes are not crimes committed by politicians. Infact, it is not defined in any statutes. Treason, sedition, espionage, other acts of endangering the external security of the State, rebellion and incitement to civil war are all viewed as offences exclusively against the sovereign authority and are considered as pure political offences—says Kittrie.

252

Political crimes are of two kinds-namely "pure political crimes" and "complex or connected offences". Pure political crimes may be seen under 251 above. Offences that endanger the life and property of individuals but are carried out in connection with and in furtherance of a crime against the State are called complex or connected to political offences.

253

Crimes like murder, theft, robbery, corruption etc.

committed by politicians are not considered as political crimes, rather they are called common crimes.

254

Political crimes may be a passing event or a deed; but terrorism is a process, a way of life, a dedication—says D.C. Rapoport.

255

A terrorist is distinguished from a political offender on the basis of the nature of his deeds, strategy of actions and goals. A political offender is not necessarily committed to violence. During the course of his activities, violence may erupt as a result of an incident or misunderstanding which may momentarily inflame the persons involved in the activities.

256

A true terrorist consciously and wilfully employs terror with an intention to spread panic by optimizing uncertainty.

257

The strategy of the terrorist is to resort to the quickest and the surest way of destroying the whole filthy order—says Nachayeff. The strategy of action usually is to attack the masses — "the very people they want to liberate, but to attack them in such a way that it is the government which appears to be their enemy" — adds Rapoport.

258

What can the police do with terrorism ? All criminal deeds committed by terrorists should be dealt with in accordance to the provisions of the penal statutes. The terrorists should be prosecuted, tried and punished. The police have nothing more to do here.

259

Police may realize that terrorism has political, social, economic and similar causes for its erruption and development. Hence, the problem should be dealt with politically, socially or economically as the case is.

260

Alcoholism is not a police problem. It is a medical problem. For, alcoholism is the effect of excessive intake of alcohol on the functioning of the body and personality. The range at the mental level is all the way from inflation of ego and loss of control to hallucination and dementia; at the physical level, from depression to degeneration; at the social level, from impaired functioning to derelict states—say W.C. Reckless. If it is so, how can it be a police problem ?

261

What is the relationship between alcoholism and criminality. There is no relation at all as an alcoholic cannot commit crimes. Disorderly conduct, vagrancy etc. may be committed by him. They cannot be treated as crimes of grave nature.

262

Alcoholism - and - under the influence of alcohol: both are two things and should not be confused. A person may commit crimes under the influence of alcohol and if that is the case, he should be dealt with accordingly. Section 85 of the Indian Penal Code— 1860 reads: "Nothing is an offence which is done by a person who, at the time of doing it, is by reason of intoxication, incapable of knowing the nature of the act, or that he is doing what is either wrong or contrary to law provided that the thing which intoxicated him was administered to him without his knowledge or against his will".

263

Any person who commits a crime under intoxication is also guided by section 86 of the Indian Penal Code— 1860 which reads : "In cases where an act done is not an offence unless done with a particular knowledge or intent, a person who does the act in a state of intoxication shall be liable to be dealt with as if he had the same knowledge as he would have had if he had not been intoxicated, unless the thing which intoxicated, him was administered to him without his knowledge or against his will".

GOD'S MOST
BEAUTIFUL CREATION
AND
MOST VULNERABLE TOO
TO BECOME VICTIMS
OF CRIME

264

Alcoholism has four stages — namely pre-alcoholic symptomatic phase, the prodromal phase, the crucial phase and the chronic phase — of development. Earlier stages of alcoholism is associated with crime and the later stages are not. During the later stages of alcoholism, one cannot commit crimes and therefore there is no earthly utility in dealing with an alcoholic by the police. Let him go to a treatment centre or advise him to get treated for alcoholism and that is what the police can or should do with an alcoholic.

265

Prostitution is mildly called 'Flesh Trade' or 'sexual recreation'. It is an act of sexual intercourse characterised by barter, promiscuity and emotional indifference' — says Encyclopaedia of Social Sciences. Is prostitution a police problem? It is not, yet the police can do something to prevent it if they want it.

266

Poverty can never be a cause of prostitution. For rich girls too go as call girls and old women, if at all they are very poor, cannot become prostitutes. It is nothing but commercilizing sex for making easy money by girls who do not have any sex values. Many girls who go for prostitution do not suffer from absolute poverty, rather they are relatively poor.

267

There are push-factors and pull-factors for girls to become prostitutes. Easy money making may be a pull factor.

268

In raiding brothels, police should maintain absolute dignity. Never enter a brothel without knocking at the door and never touch a woman when arresting her by a male officer. Let women police do all those things—such as arrest and safe custody etc. Otherwise mud may stick.

269

Are there male prostitutes ? No, they are called homosexuals. They may indulge themselves in mutual masturbation. Some good looking boys are predisposed to become 'prostitutes' because their appearance attracts particular type of homosexuals.

270

Who are these pimps and panderers ? "Pimps" are people who live from the earnings of prostitutes and "Panderers" are those who recruit, encourage or coerce girls and women to become prostitutes.

271

Police cannot really suppress the practice of prostitution so long as the demand and supply exist. Police can not do away with the practice without removing or erradicating the causes of prostitution. Then what to do ? All over the world, there exist segregated areas for prostitutes, licensing through medical inspection, protection of prostitutes from exploitation and providing of adequate health education for prostitutes and for the people around.

272

There are a number of non-police agencies providing services to help prostitutes and for their rehabilitation. Why not police co-operate with such non-governmental organizations for erradicating (controlling) prostitution ?

273

White collar crime is a violation of criminal law by a person of the upper socio-economic class in the course of his occupational activities — Says Edwin H. Surtherland. White collar criminals are not usually handled by policemen as they are normally handled by senior officers who are also said to enjoy similar status as the white collar criminals themselves.

274

There is no reason to think that the medical men, lawyers, businessmen, police officers, chartered accountants who indulge in committing white collar crimes suffer from mental disorders, manias or phobias. They are men of affairs and position and therefore a policeman can do little or very little against such sharks in society. How should the policeman fight against white collar criminals ? How should the law be enacted to control, prevent or suppress this evil ? Are the laws in India adequate to deal with the problem ? All these are issues for debate now.

275

'Drug addiction is the state of periodic and chronic intoxication detrimental to individual and to the society produced by repeated consumption of a drug—either natural or synthetic (World Health Organization). Basically, addiction is a medical problem and therefore is not a police problem. At the same time, trafficking in narcotics is a police problem.

276

The relationship between drug addiction and commission of crime is not very clear. There are many studies which show that there is no clear relationship between the two. Ofcourse, illegal manufacture, possession or sale of drugs etc. are crimes, but they are of different nature.

277

Police action to control drug addiction is often difficult, if not impossible. Yet, they can try to enforce the prohibition laws against possessing, taking, selling, manufacturing, trafficking etc. of drugs.

278

Gambling is a game of chance and people gamble. Gambling in a private house is not an offence in India. Enforcement of laws and implementation of punishments to gamblers seem to be very difficult. One of the reasons is that the gambling organizations include highly placed political people, police and other law-enforcement officers. Something can be done only if there is a strong will and determination.

279

Organised crime is described as ".....the product of a self perpetuating criminal conspiracy to wring exorbitant profits from our society by means—fair and foul, legal and illegal. Despite personnel changes, the conspiratorial entity continues. It is a malignant parasite which fattens on human weakness. It survives on fear and corruption. By one or another means, it obtains a high degree of immunity from the law. It is a totalitarian organization, a way of life that imposes rigid discipline on underlings who do the dirty work while the top men of the organization are insulated from the criminal act and the consequent danger of prosecution" (R. Salerno & J.S. Tompkins). Lower level police are helpless to initiate any stringent action against organised criminals as some of the top-level police officers get regular "payments" from syndicate-criminals. There is seen some sort of unofficial approval of the organized criminality by the so called law—enforcement officers and political leadership.

280

Controlling the crime-syndicate means controlling the rich and the affluent, the powerful and the influential in society. Yet, a more committed and vigorous law enforcement officer can do a lot to control organised crimes. Will it be ever possible ? Let us see !

281

Prison is a "place properly arranged and equipped to the reception of persons who by legal process are committed to it for safe custody while awaiting trial or for punishment (Vidyabhushan). This may be an old definition of prisons. Today, prisons are no more considered as punishment centres. They are centres of correction and the prison officials should have this thinking more than any other.

282

Prisons should not be considered as detention centres for those who await trial. Those who await trial are yet to be proved that they committed the offence. They do not, infact, deserve to be treated like the inmates in a correctional institution with (as it is) penal approaches and food.

283

Almost $^{3}/_{4}$th of the prison population are remand-prisoners in some States in India. They stay in the prisons for months and years together awaiting trial. After the trial, when they are adjudged to be innocent (if that is the case), then the sufferings they underwent in the prisons becomes sufferings for nothing. Who is more guilty here ? The enforcement officers or the so named "guilty" ? Victimological compensation should be awarded in such cases.

284

What is this? Inadequate food, loathsome sanitary conditions, lack of proper care and supervision, ill-clothings and improper medical facilities prevailed in Indian prisons — These observations were made by several jail committees and all of them wanted changes. Still the situations are not improved although many say conditions of the prisoners in India have improved a lot.

285

Corporal punishments are not allowed in prisons, yet the inmates of Indian prisons complain of them. Why ? "Corporal punishment brutalizes the offender and executioner alike. It breeds hatred and bitterness, uproots personal dignity and frustrates any attempt at social readjustment" (I.P.P.C).

286

The inmates in correctional institutions are not altogether devoid of human values. A good many among the inmates observe religious rites. They devote time for prayer. They help one another and share their joys and sorrows. Any correctional institution represents the qualities of the people outside the institutional walls. But, many an authority fails or refuses to accept these realities.

287

Correctional ideals and reformatory philosophy may remain as cliche-ridden expressions unless the police and prison officials do not possess adequate aptitude and requisite orientation or professional competence to execute the policy and programmes. They should have human considerations, empathy and understanding.

CRIME IS AS OLD AS HUMANITY
Adam and Eve violated God's commands and thus they committed the first crime –says the Holy Bible.
And Demon's instigation was said to be the cause of crime. The search for the etiology of crime is also as old as humanity.

288

Is the life in prisons meant only to carry out the 'fiat' of court judgements ? Is it a means to reform and correct an erred citizen ? It seems that there exists confusion in this area. Penologists may say that measures to correct a crime-doer should start at the moment he is caught by the police, should be continued during the stages of prosecution and trial and later should be positively pursued when he is confined in the correctional institution. Is this possible ? Is it practicable ? Is it desirable ? A lot of confusion exists.

289

Basic procedural safeguards such as the presumption of innocence, the right to be notified of the charges, the right to remain silent, the right to counsel, the right to the presence of a parent/guardian, the right to confront and cross-examine witnesses and the right to appeal to a higher authority are internationally accepted guarantees to the suspects/accused/crime-doers at all stages of proceedings. Accept them as they are.

290

A juvenile offender caught by the police has a right to privacy. It should be respected at all stages of criminal proceedings. No undue publicity or harm should be offered to the juveniles apprehended. No information which may lead to the identification of a juvenile offender should be published.

291

Any human act can be interpretted as a crime with some justifications. For, the penal laws are so comprehensive that an interpretation may appear to be correct also. But, before interpreting an act, the police may look — (1) the seriousness of the act, (2) frequency of occurrences of such a behaviour and (3) the attitude of the crime-doer to his act. This is very important particularly when children are involved.

292

Broken homes, slum-life, motion-pictures, obscene literature, family disorganisation, divorce, disertion, unemployment, overcrowding, illegitimacy, orphanhood, undesirable conditions at home, quarrels, intoxication, immorality, poverty, lack of care and control and many such factors may be indirectly responsible for causing delinquency among children. Unhappy home, too harsh or too lax home atmosphere, authoritatian or permissive parent, lack of family solidarity, parental discrimination etc. may further result in delinquent behaviour. Each delinquent or neglected child is a case-study in himself or herself.

293

Crime movies, sex-stimulating scenes, false adventurism, untrue criminal heroism, delinquent behaviour etc. may create delinquency. Films teach and children learn what is being taught.

294

What are the police roles in the prevention of delinquency ? They are—

1. discovery of juvenile delinquents, potential delinquents and conditions inducing delinquency.
2. investigation of individual cases involving juveniles and youthful offenders
3. providing a constructive solutions for individual cases and conditions inducting delinquency and
4. providing an overall effective control operations which may protect children and reduce opportunities for commission of law violations by juveniles (Kenney & Pursuit).

What are the roles of police in the prevention and rehabilitation of juvenile delinquents ? They are—

1. stopping the tendencies toward deviant behaviour in children before deviancy occurs
2. checking misbehaviour from becoming worse or more frequent
3. treating of delinquents and predelinquents, neglected and abused children
4. attempting to eliminate or atleast curtail the extent of the underlying causes of deviation. (Kenney and Pursuit).

296

Police policy and approach to juveniles should always emphasise the well-being of the children. Care, protection, welfare, education, safety, correction, rehabilitation etc. should be the guiding force behind juvenile justice.

297

In order to best fulfil their functions, police officer who frequently or exclusively deal with juveniles or who are primarily engaged in the prevention of juvenile crime shall be specifically instructed and trained. In large cities, special police units should be established (U.N's S M R For Administration of Juvenile Justice).

298

All police lock-ups should meet all requirements of health of the detainees. There should be sufficient place for the detainees to sleep during night hours and it should have enough cubic content of air. There should be constant and continuous supervision over the detainees so kept in police lock-ups.

299

Every police station should have adequate bathing and toilet facilities for the detainees to make use of them whenever they want.

300

At usual hours, every detainee should be provided with food or should be allowed to have food at his cost. Starvation in police lock-ups is a henious sin committed against the suspects/ detainees.

301

Every detainee in police lock-up should be informed of his rights and privileges. He should also be informed of the disciplinary requirements in police stations.

302

Every detainee in police lock-up is a suspect and should be treated as such. He should be allowed to wear his own clothing

TRAIN SABOTAGE

This is a scene of a passenger train accident. Some people are killed and many are injured.

People gather there for rescue operations and some of them plunder the injured and the dead.

Protecting the scene of accident is a real problem for the police.

WHAT A STRANGE PSYCHOLOGY INDEED !

and under no circumstance, he should be compelled to remain only in underclothings or in humiliating dress.

303

A detainee in a police lock-up should be permitted to apply for free legal aid where such legal aid is available and to receive visits from his lawyer. Ofcourse, the interviews between him and his lawyer may be within the sight of the police authorities but not within the hearing of police officials.

304

Women detainees shall never be kept in police lock-ups during night hours—i.e., after sun-set and before sunrise.

305

Women detainees shall never be kept along with men detinues in police lock-ups during day time.

306

Whenever women detainees are kept in police custody, all facilities for their monthly—mensural periods—care should be provided if that needs be.

CHAPTER - 3

CRIME AND CRIMINAL JUSTICE : IS CRIME ABNORMAL ?

307

Many a criminal, when he is caught, feels that he has committed a blunder.

308

Many a criminal, when he is acquitted by a court of law, laughs at the follies and blunders committed by police and prosecutor.

309

Many a criminal, when he is interrogated, resorts to all kinds of defence mechanisms to escape from the mental conflicts.

310

Crime is a crime inspite of its gravity.

311

Police officers relish catching of criminals and criminals prefer escape from the police.

312

Some police officers think that the criminals are fools, but many criminals know that a good many police officers are not intelligent enough to take advantage of the foolery they have done while committing the offences.

313

Many crime-doers thank the police department that they were not caught earlier.

PRINT MEDIA AND CRIMES

Thirty to forty per cent of the daily newspapers brings out the news and views about crimes. They influence the people to become criminals. Even juveniles are attracted.

The periodicals bring stories of crime and they speak more of emotions than of reason. People read and they enjoy.

Media teaches and the people learn.

314

Never judge a crime-doer by his look; he may be prettier than many others in the world.

315

No criminal wants to make a confession of his crime to a police officer, but he may if he is forced to. Ofcourse the police may succeed in making a person to shut his eyes, but they can not make him sleep. Never coerce a man to make confessions. It is illegal, unethical and unnecessary.

316

The police may envy a criminal when they know the amount and area of fortune he makes by his criminal career, but if the police were to know how he makes them, surely he will be pitied.

317

Why people commit crimes ? How do they commit them ? It is better that one should not know them, for, facts are sometimes stranger than fiction. How do the police detect the crime and the criminal ? — How do they handle the criminals and prove the crime against them ? It is better that one should not know them, for, here too facts are stranger than fiction. What do the accused do to get acquittal verdicts or how they are convicted ? — Here too facts are stranger than fiction.

318

"Father, forgive them; for they know not what they do"—This is the prayer of Jesus Christ on the Cross and He prayed so to his Father in Heaven seeing the way law is enforced against Him by the then enforcement machinery. Is the same condition prevail and continue now ? Do the crime-doers pray so in police stations ? — in correctional institutions ?

319

Crimes become very grave when motives behind the detection and interpretation become anything other than administration of justice.

320

Fear ensures intelligence even to a hard-core criminal. Confessions are made out of fear, no matter the one who confesses is or is not the real culprit. Avoid coercion during interrogation.

321

Let one thousand criminals go unpunished — no innocent man should be punished. This may be a chiche-ridden expression. Now the thinking is : 'Let all the thousand criminals be punished and never allow an innocent man to suffer the punishment'. Inspite of it, conviction rate is going down alarmingly all over the country. Why ?

322

Fish and guests smell in 24 hours. Every detainee in a police station is a guest. Ensure the Constitutional guarantees to all the detinues in police lock-ups.

323

A criminal's wisdom may be a folly before the police and the wisdom of the police can also be a folly before the criminal.

324

Only man weaps or better can weap. See the tears in the eyes of the suspect, in the eyes of the victims of his crime and in the eyes of the dependents of the suspect before taking any decision as to what to do or how to go about in handling a crime-doer.

325

Only man, among the living beings, makes prayers and if they are made by a criminal, listen to him attentively. He has no one else to pray, for, the police interrogator is his "god" at that moment of misery and stress.

326

'Opportunity makes the thief' — This is an English proverb. Is this statement true in all sorts of crimes ?

327

Every criminal speaks the same thing in the same way in different languages in all cultures, in all countries and throughout the human history. He may try to justify his act and there is justification for everything he does or did.

328

Crimes people commit are before the eyes of the police and the same of the police are behind their backs or under the earth. Khakhi collar crimes are also crimes under the existing penal laws of the common-man.

329

Crimes often committed by police usually irritate them most when they see the same in others. They then become law-keepers, executors of law, moralists, philosophers, social welfare workers and what not ?

330

A suspect and a police-interrogator are hostile to each other. They do not trust each other. The suspect cann't and the police won't.

331

Only a fool of the first order will test the depth of water with both feet—This is a Malayalam proverb. And, likewise, only a fool will confess to the police of his involvement in crimes. Hence interrogate a suspect only with convincing evidence.

332

One thing the policemen can't understand about criminals is, how the criminals understand so much about them and another thing the criminals do not understand is, how the policemen understand so much about them. Both are superior to each other and suspicious too.

333

One of the strangest things about the policemen is that those who want to administer justice can not do so because of interferences, introductions and recommendations.

ELECTRONIC MEDIA AND CRIMES

Mini screens, cables, video-tapes bring out crimes of violence, sex stimulating scenes, fooling the police, making easy money, suicidal deaths, aggression, erotic conversation, false heroism, untrue stories etc. etc., and the people who enjoy them—having weak ego-structure—are influenced by the visual media and thus they commit crimes or become victims of crimes.

SEEING IS BELIEVING

334

One policeman can take care of many people in society, but many people in society can not take care of one policeman. Attacks on police is on the increase and corruption too.

335

One reason why a criminal is such a hated creature in society is that nobody is prepared to listen patiently his version of the crime. The victims of crime may be as culpable as the criminal himself.

336

One crime is enough for a criminal to be branded as a 'criminal afterall' all throughout his life.

337

One eye-witness is better than a hundred ear-withnesses to a crime.

338

One law for the handicapped and another for the affluent ! There should not be discrimination in law enforcement or execution.

339

One moment of patience may ward off great disaster; one moment of impatience may ruin a whole life. Impatience is said to be the root cause of custodial violence. Is it true ?

340

One must commit a crime and suffer its consequences to know the luxury of not becoming a criminal and of not being caught as a crime-doer.

341

Often, a criminal of criminals lives like a king of kings, but lies unseen by many in society. Boss in organised criminality or crime syndicates is really an emperor in his world and in the underworld.

342

Omlets are not made without breaking the egg-shells. Likewise, a person should not be caught for breaking the laws if he does not. Avoid registering of false cases.

343

Do not bite a thing till you know whether it is a cake or iron. Logically, do not treat a person as a criminal until you know that he has really committed a crime and then try to understand him.

344

Do not treat a person to be a criminal until he is proved to have committed an offence.

345

A crime should not surprise a police officer, for, he is meant to deal with it. Crimes are also human acts.

346

Descend a step to interrogate a suspect in a crime and ascend a step to charge-sheet him as an accused. Show nobility and character even in accusing people. Never concoct evidence for getting a conviction to the chargesheeted.

347

Punishment to a real criminal can be deferred, but can never be prevented. It may come to him in some form or another-may not be from the police or from the court. Nature has its own punishments.

348

Dignity is something that can not be preserved in corruption. Allegations against corrupt investigation bring distrust of police sense of justice.

349

Do not think that something is achieved by getting a person convicted. The achievement lies in making him or converting him to a law abiding citizen.

350

Drown not thyself to save the life of a drowning man—this is an English proverb. Likewise, never commit a crime to prove a crime committed by another.

351

Crime is an expression of the superiority of the criminal. Accept it.

352

Even a hair has its own shadow. Likewise, a petty criminal has his own version of his act. Listen to it.

353

Some police officers complain that the suspect is not co-operating with them during interrogation. What do they mean by 'co-operation'? Co-operate to see that the interrogated goes to jail ?

129

Both the police officer and the crime-doer—are God's images and God knows what is wrong with each one of them.

355

Every crime has its beauty and every criminal has his too. Never hate a crime and a crime-doer. They also have a purpose to be fulfilled in this spectacular world.

356

Police interrogation is intolerable to a criminal who is best prepared to answer the questions in the most honest way, for, the most foolish interrogator can ask any questions which the wisest man on earth can not answer and in every answer he can find out something suspicious.

357

Every police interrogator is an intelligent man. For, the law has empowered him to question an intelligent suspect. If he uses muscles to interrogate a crime-doer, it means that he is definitely inferior to the interrogated.

DEATH PENALTY
IS NO PUNISHMENT
IT IS NOT A SOLUTION TO CRIME

358

A police interrogator who uses muscles to question a suspect is a coward, for, he can show his power and strength only when he wears the uniform. Let him remove his uniform and show his muscle and then he can know who is who and what is what. Never manhandle a suspect when he is in police custody—and that too during an interrogation.

359

Many suspects succeed during police interrogation because they are able to appear like fools and they can behave like wise-men.

360

If a policeman in a police station smiles at you, look the other way—some criminals say so. The smile may be either to catch them or to cash on them—They add further.

361

If a man dies in police custody, there is no need to call it to be a suicide. Deaths in police custody, all over the world, throughout centuries, are suicides unless proved otherwise.

362

If a suspect wonders at the wonderful treatments he received in a police station, no doubt, the treatments were wonderful—If he feels contempt, they were contemptuous--If he feels fair and just, doubtlessly, they were fair and just. The suspect in a crime is the best judge of how he is treated in a police station.

363

If a police officer sees a path with no obstacles during an investigation, it probably leads to the acquittal of the case in a court of law.

364

If a police officer has collected no evidence against a suspect, do not question him. For, by questioning, one can create suspicion about anyone. No man on earth will be able to answer all

THE LAST WISH

The verdict was to hang the murderer until he dies.....

Just before the execution, the officials asked : "What is your last desire ?"

The convict, very politely, said : "Sir, I may be permitted to kiss your sweet wife."

The officer got irritated. He was infuriated and then became wild. He uttered : "Hang him immediately. He wants to kiss my wife. Rascal !"

The convict smiled at the comments of the officer and said:

"Sir, I requested you to permit me to kiss your wife—and it is my last desire. Instead of saying YES or NO to my request, you became angry and ordered to hang me immediately. Sir, please remember that mine is a request—the request of a convict who is waiting for the rope at the bottom of the gallows." He further said : "If my last wish, remaining at the foot of the gallows, has made you to be infuriated to this extent—to the pronouncing of a merciless order-, then may I know why I am punished to be hanged for killing the seducer of my wife when I saw him doing it ?"

Surely, it is a question to the LAW, LEGAL SYSTEM and ADMINISTRATION OF JUSTICE.

MORAL OF THE STORY—EVERYBODY may become infuriated in similar situations and such people deserve sympathy, consideration and understanding.

IF PENALTY IS TO REFORM THE CRIME-DOER, THEN DEATH PENALTY ANNIHILATES THE CRIMINAL. THE PURPOSE OF PUNISHMENT IS DEFEATED.

questions in an honest way and there is no need for anyone to be that honest to police officers.

365

Human rights are sacred rights. They are the birth rights of all human beings. These inalienable rights should not be violated by the police. Many police officers/men know it. But, maximum number of complaints on violations of human rights are received against the police and it is really bad.

366

If a police officer wants to know how he performs his job, ask several people to speak more about how his subordinates do. The answers to the questions will be a true picture of how he is. If they are late to the office, it means that he too is late. If they are corrupt, it means that he too is and thus it goes......

367

Crimes are crimes and criminals are criminals. But, if you speak insults to the criminals, you will also hear them. You are no better than the criminal you deal with.

368

If you want to know the bad points of your superior, then praise him to another superior officer equal or higher in rank to him. He will then say that he has more of criminal tendencies and undersirable personality traits.

369

Petty cases, petty crimes, petty criminals—and you are not meant to book such 'petties'. You are also becoming petty when you register more of petty cases.

370

Look at a human being in the police lock-up and see whether or not he smiles at you. If you see that he can not 'smile at you, it means that he can not smile. Why, give him your smile and let us see whether or not it makes any difference.

371

If you pick up a real culprit and make him an accused, then he will not say anything against you and that is the difference between a real offender and an innocent man. Never register false cases and charge-sheet innocent people.

372

If you sin against a sinner more than his sinning, you can not escape miseries. Every sinner has some psychic powers which invoke justice on the sinner against him !

373

If you want to keep good relations with your superiors, go to him with a telescope and never with a microscope. If you want to know more about crimes and criminals, approach them with a microscope and not with a telescope. Never try to establish too much friendly relations with superiors and criminals.

374

Good relations with a criminal may be exploited and the same with superiors will be misused. Beware of the evil consequences !!

375

Ill-won money, ill-gotten fame, ill-captured position and ill-earned friends never stick. Corruption, deception, exercise of pseudo-authority etc. should be avoided.

376

In a police lock-up, one can see a station-house officer's thoughts and there only one will see them. Every detainee will say whether or not, the staff in the station are more concerned about him or themselves !

377

In police interrogation, the facts are not counted—say the policeman. And in every police interrogation, the fists alone are counted—say human rights activists.

378

Inside every real culprit, there is an intelligent criminal trying to get out. Be careful about various defence mechanisms resorted to by the interrogated during police interrogation.

379

He is a bad interrogator who brings the dependents, kith and kin, parents and so on to exert pressure on the offenders to confess their guilt. It is still worse to humiliate, harass, victimize or pressure such innocent people. Conduct interrogation only after collection of evidence against the offenders.

380

It is a great secret worth knowing that police officers seldom go to police stations with their own cases. Why ? And there lies the secret of police service.

381

A police officer was asked : "Do you have any guilt feelings when you understand that you had wrongly roughed up an innocent person in your custody ?" In reply, he said : "I had guilt feelings during the initial stages of my entry into police service. Now, it is about 12 years I am on the job and what is there to feel guilty about my acts ?" Yes, there is a point in what he says too.

382

The rule is that women should be interrogated by a police officer infront of another woman. The interrogation by male police officers—though in the presence of women police—is not free from coercion, threat, abuse or torture. Allegations are sometimes raised that the women constables silently connive with their male counterparts—particularly superior officers—to question women suspects even by employing third degree methods. Is the allegation true ?

383

'It is no honour for an eagle to vanquish a dove'—This is a wise saying. Is it an honour for a police officer to get a confession from a suspect by threat, false promises, exercise of pseudo-authority, manhandling or misuse of power ?

TRUANCY

A TRUANT IS A STUDENT WHO STAYS AWAY FROM SCHOOL WITHOUT PERMISSION (THE RANDOM HOUSE COLLEGE DICTIONARY)

"I SAW THE ANGEL IN THE MARBLE AND I JUST CHISELLED TILL I SET HIM FREE"—(Michelangelo). Likewise, if the parents, teachers, preachers and people can see and acknowledge the greatness in children truancy can be reduced.

384

It is not the police actions on a criminal that make him afraid of the police—it is rather the fear of going to a police station, of being treated by the police inside and outside the police lock-up and later the stories people around him may speak of.

385

It is not how long an interrogation is conducted is important; it is how well it is done.

386

It is not muscles, stamina and physique which make the police a service. They make the police a force and not a service.

387

There is no meaning in giving a sermon on morality to immoral people, goodness to evil people and saintliness to sinners. This is not right, for both the police and criminals require sermons as people have a potency to become moral, good and saintly. Sinners have become saints and saints have become sinners. Best wishes!

388

Police, at times, violate laws to execute laws. It is plain madness to do so, for, the wise saying is "it is plain madness to live in want that you may die rich".

389

It is the police officer who makes mistakes, and not the theories of crime, crime causation and scientific methods of investigation. They are laborious, time-consuming and pain-staking to understand a crime and a criminal in a scientific way.

390

It is the police interrogator who has no evidence that kicks the suspects—just like a cow which has no milk kicks the one who milks it.

391

Lack of intelligence is the root of all failures in detection, arrest, interrogation, prosecution, trial, correction and rehabilitation of a criminal.

392

"Law catches flies, but lets hornets go free"--This is a wise saying and test the truth of it in police work.

393

'Learning makes a good man better and an ill man worse'—This is an English proverb. It is true in the case of criminals as well as policemen. Policemen too learn the crooked ways by association and contacts with other policemen who have learnt them from other policemen who had similar study and learning.

394

Virtue is what a police officer wants to see in a criminal and that is what he too should have in himself to be a good police officer.

395

Living without committing crimes is almost impossible—no, impossible indeed.

396

Interrogation is a wonderful experience. It teaches the interrogator and the interrogated steadfastness, patience, broad-mindedness, sympathy, consideration, tolerance, understanding and a lot of other things which would not be needed if they were not the interrogator and the interrogated.

397

Modes and methods may change—but human nature is the same. It is true in committing crimes, fooling police and escaping punishments.

398

Most nurses are sweet girls who hold the wrist and expect

normal pulse. It is possible ? Yes, it is—many a time with women patients and old people. Most police officers are smart people who question the suspects to get true answers. It is possible ? Yes, it is—many a time with people who have prepared themselves to go to jail after their confessions.

399

Most of the real criminals enjoy the inferiority of the police department--For, it is because of it that they are not detected and caught.

400

'Nature does nothing invain'—(English Proverb) and man too does nothing invain. A criminal does nothing invain and so does a policeman. A prosecutor does nothing invain and so is a court of law and the criminal goes to jail. A jailor does nothing invain and so does an appellate court and the convicted criminal goes out of the jail. Everyone does everything for ensuring justice and everyone sees what indeed is justice !

401

'Necessity knows no law'--(Latin Proverb) and criminal knows no law when he commits a crime out of necessity.

402

Need makes the naked man run and a police officer is no exception to it when pressures are exerted on him to detect a crime and arrest the criminal on a need based investigation. Need ? — Justice ? —Need for Justice ? —All these are questions not answered at that time.

403

Never accuse a criminal for the crime he committed. For, your own crimes may be graver than what he has done. Try to correct the wrong doer.

404

One can not correct a crime—but can always correct a crime-doer or the situations causing crimes. If you correct a crime, the act ceases to be a crime and then there will be no criminals at all.

CONDUCT DISORDER — UNDERSOCIALIZED AGGRESSIVE

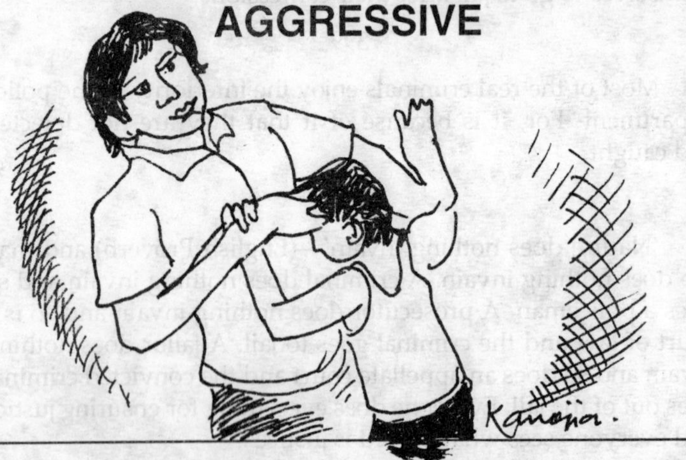

CONDUCT DISORDER–Undersocialized Aggressive

Diagnostic criteria

A repetitive and persistent pattern of aggressive conduct in which the basic rights of others are violated, as manifested by either of the following–

(1) Physical violance against persons or property : e.g. vandalism, rape, breaking and entering, fire setting, mugging, assault

(2) Thefts outside the home involving confrontation with the victim (e.g.) extortion, purse-snatching, armed robbery)

Failure to establish a normal degree of affection, empathy, or bond with others as evidenced by no more than one of the following indications of social attachment :

(i) has one or more peer group friendships that have lasted over six months

(ii) extends himself or herself for others even when no immediate advantage is likely.

(iii) apparently feels guilt or remorse when such a reaction is appropriate (not just when caught or in difficulty)

(iv) avoids blaming or informing on companions

(v) shares concern for the welfare of friends or companions. (from D.S.M. III).

405

Never trust a lawyer too far and a policeman too near. Both are people interested in administration of justice and they may do anything if you keep too far from the lawyer or too close to the policeman—and they do everything in the name of administering justice !

406

Suspects sleep in police lock-ups. Are they so tired that they can not but sleep ? Are they not worried about the after-effects of their stay in the police lock-up? 'No pillow is as soft as a clean conscience'— is this French Proverb applicable to their behaviour ? Think......think and think of it before the next interrogation session begins.

407

No one thinks of committing a crime until he gets a chance to do so.

408

No one committing a crimes wants to be caught.

409

'Nothing is good or bad, but thinking makes it so'– (English Proverb) and it is true even with respect to crimes and criminal behaviours.

CHAPTER - 4

CRIME AND POLICE : IS THE POLICE ABLE TO CONTROL CRIMES?

410

The causative forces which operate on women to commit crimes are the same which work on men. Crimes committed by women and the crimes committed against women are not many as they are evidenced by the statistics available. Women enjoy more rights, by virtue of the sex, than men when they are handled by police. Hence the police are expected to offer all safeguards and protection to women when they are handled. Otherwise, mud may stick.

411

Women should not be called to police stations for investigation. All police investigations, as far as possible, must be carried out in the presence of a relative of the accused or her lawyer and of a lady staff member— This is a recommendation of Mulla committee.

412

Women in police custody should invariably be under the charge of women police officials. No undue influence shall be exerted on such police officials by senior levels so that they do not object to what is being done on women by male police officials. Women police officials should be free to protect the women suspects/detainees under police custody.

413

Pregnant women or nursing women under police custody should be provided with special diet. All necessary arrangements

SEX-CRIMES : DICTIONARY

Adamism	:	A form of exhibitionism in which the subject exhibits himself in the nude.
Algolagnia	:	Synonymous with sado-masochism. Active algolagnia being sadism; passive algolagnia being masochism.
Anlagen	:	Genetic predisposition.
Anilingus	:	Sexual pleasure obtained through the use of the mouth or the anus.
Auto-Eroticism	:	Sexual love or fixation on oneself.
Beastiality	:	Sexual intercourse with animals.
Bisexuality	:	Erotic inclination or capacity to both sexes existing in one individual.
Coitus	:	Sexual intercourse.
Cunnilingus	:	Apposition of the tongue or mouth to the vulva; oral copulation.
Diana Complex	:	A psychological reaction found among young females, sometimes referred to as 'VIRILITY COMPLEX'.
Electra Complex	:	Sexual desire of the daughter towards her father, with hostility towards her mother.
Enuritics	:	Psychpaths who are interested in urine.
Exhibitionism	:	(Spectacular Complex) The exposure of the genitalia for the purpose of sexual gratification; the genitalia is usually in a condition of excitement; the act is more prevelent among males.

(Continued.......)

From *Crime and the Sexual Psychopath*
by Paul De River

Examine your own conscience. Did you ever have a sex problem which disturbed you? If you did not have any, it shows that something is wrong with your sexual development. Consult a doctor.

should be provided for medical consultation for them, if that needs be.

414

Bail should be liberally granted to women. Special consideration should be shown to women for answering their nature's call and mensural necessities when they are in police custody.

415

Women shall not be arrested between sun set and sun rise and shall not be arrested except in the presence of other women.

416

In all cases of bailable offences, bail on her bond shall be granted forthwith by the police themselves. As far as possible, in non-bailable cases also, bail should be granted unless special circumstances warrant a different course, in which case, the arrested women shall be remanded to judicial custody with utmost expedition — suggest the National Commission for Women.

417

On arrest, the police should immediately obtain from the woman arrestee the name of a relative or friend to whom the intimation of her arrest should be promptly given. Showing some address as if it is furnished by the woman arrestee and sending to such addressee the intimation of arrest may not be resorted to as the procedure is unethical and blame-worthy.

418

Showing on the record that a woman has been arrested after sun-rise and before sun set—when the fact is otherwise—is a misuse of authority. Further, showing that the woman is arrested in the presence of another woman—when the fact is not true is immoral, and unjustifiable and tantamounts to misuse of authority.

419

The person of the woman shall not be searched except by a woman duly authorized by law and in a manner strictly in accordance with the requirements of decency. Respect should be shown to the womanhood even when she is being searched by another woman. Whenever women police officers search the person of another woman, that should be done, away from the sight of men police officers. In cases, when the person/body of a woman is searched by another woman (not a woman police officer), then facilities should be provided to do the same in isolation — away from the presence of men police officers.

420

Whether in custody or in transit, the woman arrestee should be guarded by a police woman or a female surrogate. Even here, a subordinate police woman may be handicapped to raise her voice against superior police officer's doings (and misdoings?). As a precaution against an allegation likely to be raised, it is advisable to permit a relative of the woman arrestee to accompany her while escorting her.

421

There are any number of allegations against male police officers for molestation of woman in police custody and custodial rape. There is public distrust of police and as such, any safeguards, precautions, protections taken to ensure that the women are handled, treated and dealt with decently will not be too much. The burden of showing to the women and to the public that female arrestees and offenders are treated well lies on the shoulders of police.

422

Whenever a woman is to be examined by the police or other investigative agency as a witness, it should be done at her residence or at a place where she is likely to be found. There shall not be any discrimination on this count basing on the status, financial positions, caste-considerations or anything of similar nature.

423

No woman - witness shall be summoned to the police or investigative station unless she expresses her preference to be examined in a police station. Creating of records to show that a female witness prefers to be examined in police stations—when the facts are otherwise--is unethical and unjustifiable.

424

Going to the residence of female witnesses/to the place where they are likely to be found, in police uniform or in police vehicles in a conspicuous manner so that people around the locality may take note of it is very bad. It may result in the loss of police-witness rapport. It can also cause the worsening of the human relationship of the witness to the accused/suspect/victim and so on. Hence, avoid such practices if they exist.

425

No female detinue in police custody should be hand-cuffed, fettered or remain in custody in humiliating dress. Inherent dignity of human person should be recognised.

426

Whenever a woman arrestee is detained in police custody, she should be detained in separate space for women arrestees. As far as possible, women arrestees should not be housed in police stations manned by male police officers. They should be kept in all women police stations or in lock-ups fully managed by women police officials. If such facilities are not available, then they should be kept in special home or institution designated under the law to receive women. In all such homes and institutions, the women arrestee should not be left unguarded by women guards or surrogates—suggests National Commission for Women.

427

Information on women arrestees and detainees in police custody should be made available to social organizations and individuals on request. In cases of detention of women in police custody, institutions accredited or individuals interested on such women should be allowed to visit them. Their visits should be allowed, not as a leniency, but as a matter of right to them. As a right, they should enjoy the facility to have free access to records relating to women arrestees/detainees in police stations.

428

The National Commission for Women Suggests : "In exceptional circumstances when a woman arrestee is taken to a police lock-up, the police should immediately give intimation to the nearest Legal Aid Committee or recognised legal services bodies which must render all necessary legal services at State expenses.

429

The National Commission for Women recommends: "When arresting a woman, proper arrangements for the protection and care of her children shall be the responsibility of the State. Children who need to be custodialized jointly with their mothers shall enjoy rights justly needed while in custody, in terms of food, living space, health, clothing and visitation". The police may understand that the children of the women detainees have special rights and they should be protected at any cost. As such, the police have special obligations to see that suitable arrangements for the welfare of women detainees in police custody are made for the protection of children.

430

The suspects in crimes, or the accused in trials or the detainee in police lock-ups do not lose their fundamental rights because they are so. They have fundamental and human rights as much as the police officers do enjoy. They enjoy human rights just because they are human beings and fundamental rights just because they are citizens of India.

431

The right to counsel begins when a person is being interrogated (*Nandini Sathpathy* v. *Dani*, A.I.R. 1978, S.C. 1025) and continues through pre-trial stages to trial and into appeal (*Katri* v. *Bihar*, A.I.R., 1981, S.C. 928) since it is an essential ingredient of reasonable, fair and just procedures.

432

Never humiliate a woman detinue by abusive-mouthed language or depriving them of life necessities and privacy due to a young woman particularly at certain periods of the month.

433

An offender when convicted may be fined. Fining an accused may be a source of revenue to the Government. This procedure does not ensure full justice to the victims of offence. Victimologists, therefore, suggest adequate victim compensation in every crime. There are countries where Crime Compensation Tribunals are established for this purpose. Hence, punishment to the crime-doer and compensation to the victims of crime are considered to be offering better justice. This system is called "Equal Justice System". The philosophy of Equal Justice should guide the police whenever they deal with offenders and the victims of crime.

434

Confinement to a closed, maximum security prision does not have much utility from the point of view of correction and rehabilitation of offenders. This has paved the way for open prisons which are characterized by the absence of material or physical precautions against escape. The system has proved to be a better method for correction and rehabilitation. Penologists recommend that the convicts must be sent to minimum security institutions either at the beginning of their sentence or after they have served a part of their sentence in a closed institution. The police may take note of the change in the approach to convicts. This may surely help them to have a correctional attitude to offenders when they are handled during investigation or later.

435

Probation is the suspension of sentence by a court or a conditional release from commitment to a penal institution contingent upon good behaviour (Mabel A. Elliot). Studies conducted on the success of probation show that it is the best method so far devised by society for treating of offenders. If so, the police may realize that confinement to a prison is not and should not be the end of crime-investigation.

436

Some convicts say that their sufferings in a penal institution are nothing when compared to their sufferings in police custody.

Sex-Crimes : A Dictionary

-- 2

Fallatio	:	Oral copulation—Use of mouth on the male sex organs.
Fetish	:	A symbol arousing sexual excitation-substituting of a part or article for the sexual object.
Fetishism	:	Sexual abnormality which secures sexual stimulation or gratification through some article or part of the sexual object.
Fire-Water Complex	:	Symptom seen in sexually psychopathic incerdiarists. After lighting a fire, there is a period of exhibitionism followed by a desire to urinate.
Flagellation	:	A psychosexual perversion characterised by a passion for whipping-encountered among sadomasochists—may be either active or passive.
Frotteurs	:	Addicts of a form of masturbation, closely associated with buttock fetishism. The male subject usually rubs or presses against the buttocks of a female, and sometimes a male, while in a crowd. In this condition, there is usually a homosexual element.
Gerontophilia	:	The choice of older people of the opposite sex as sexual object or partner.
Gynandry	:	The extreme grade of degenerative homosexuality in females.
Homosexuality	:	A condition in which there is a sexual fixation or erotic attachment to persons of the same sex.
Impotence	:	Lack of sexual virility.
Incest Complex	:	Desire for sexual relations with a near relative.
Invert	:	An individual with erotic inclinations towards his own sex (Homosexual)
Koprolagnia	:	A condition usually found in masochism wherein the subject is sexually excited through the senses of taste and smell by articles of filth, such as extrement (Urine and Feces)

From 'CRIME and the SEXUAL PSYCHOPATH' (op. cit)

Everybody—man and woman-has sex. Where there is sex, there may be sex aberrations. In some, it may be very projected and in some, it may not be. In some, it may be harmful to the self and to others whereas in some others, it may not be that harmful. See where you can be fitted......

If that is true, it shows that something is defective in the system and that can be removed only if the police have a will to do so.

437

Never trouble people who are granted probation by the courts.

438

Parole refers to the release of a person from a correctional facility after he has served a part of his sentence (T. Reid). Never trouble parolees unnecessarily in the pretext of criminal check or surveillance. There are parole officers appointed for the purpose.

439

"Ticket to leave" is a system by virtue of which prisoners go to their houses for a short stay. Some police officers confuse it to be 'parole' as they do not know that the parolees do not go back to jails unless they violate the conditions of parole. Those who make use of the 'ticket to leave' facility should be under the watch of police officials as they are not under parole or probation officers.

440

Probation and parole officers should be provided with all help by the police as their success in the job means reduction of crime in society. There can be co-operation and should be co-operation between the police and probation/parole officers.

441

After care services to the released prisoners must be encouraged by police. Such services often help the ex-inmates of correctional institutions for their resettlement and rehabilitation in a free society. Helping the agencies—mostly they will be non-governmental organizations—means helping to reduce crimes in society.

442

There is a general complaint for the agencies involved in after care services and it is about the non-cooperative attitude of prison authorities and police officials in their work. If it is true, surely the attitude comes from ignorance of the noble aims of after care services. Avoid such attitudes.

443

After all who is a criminal? He is an individual born as a person of inherent dignity. Hence, accept the worth of human person in all individuals. Ofcourse, he expressed a behavioural pattern unacceptable to law and society. But his behaviour is an expression of his need and it is against the law, then execute the law in the way the law says about it. Against the violation of law, there should not be violation of law.

444

Who says that an individual will not change? If you can change a world, surely a criminal too can and will change. But, for it, the right help should be given before he becomes hardened. There is no criminal who is incorrigible, and if there is, it means that the people make him to be so. And a police officer should not be a cause for the incorrigibility.

445

"Recidivism" means the habit of relapsing into crime even after incarceration in a penal institution. Why do people become recidivists? There are many reasons for it and one main reason is that the policemen often go after them to make them offenders once again—say some of the recidivists (?). Whenever a theft occurs—a burglary takes place—a pocket picking reported, immediately the police go and catch hold of the recently released inmates of prisons. If at all they repeatedly say that they are innocent, they are not believed. The result is that they confess the crimes and say: 'come, what may'.

446

Who is a recidivist? If recidivist means a repeater of crime, then every corrupt official is a recidivist. He makes corruption-money repeatedly and claims to be a law-abiding citizen. He accuses the pick pocket as a recidivist and forgets himself to be called a greater recidivist. What a deplorable state of affairs?

447

'Persistence in crime is merely a persistence of habit'—say some criminologists. They speak about drug-addiction and drunkenness as examples. They say that these habits are often initiated, formed and developed very much prior to official treatment. Ofcourse, one can understand the explanation. The question here is: "why do corrupt officials repeat their crime?" It is because, corruption has become a habit in them? Is corruption sedative?—addictive? If not, why do corrupt officials become recidivists?'

448

Prisons in modern world are called correctional institutions. Allegations are there that some prison officials are corrupt in many ways. If that is so, can correction be possible by them? If not, why call them 'correctional institutions? Recidivism means that either the correction is not 'corrective' in nature or the offender is beyond any correctional therapy. Perhaps, the first proposition is more correct than the second. Right?

449

The inmates, when they are inside the prison, are being exploited in several ways. The inmates, when they are released, go to a society where in they can commit crimes. Recidivism means that the exconvicts prefer to be exploited more in the prison than they committing crimes in society. What an attitude?

450

From the moment a person is detected to have committed an offence, he is exposed to ordeals and expenditure. As time passes by, he makes adjustments and prefers a life in confinement more than a life in freedom. Some people become recidivists because they want to be jail birds.

451

If frequent employment of third degree methods during interrogation is considered as an example for recidivism, then some of the so named law enforcement officers will be recidivists. But, they are not treated like recidivists. Surely, there exists a double standard in application here.

SEX-CRIMES : DICTIONARY

-- 3

Lust Murder : Murder committed in sadistic brutal fashion : the victim's body usually shows evidence of being mutilated particularly the genitalia.

Masochism : The correlative complex of sadism, which like its correlative, may be heterosexual or homosexual: the desire to experience pain and suffering.

Masturbation (Onanism, ipsation) Causation of sexual excitement through manual manipulation of the genitalia; auto-eroticism through friction or rubbing.

Metatrophism : The conversion of certain sexual and erotic attitudes which takes effect as masculine inclusion of the impulse life of the female, and a female inclusion of the impulse life of the male, without leading to homosexuality.

Necrofetishism : Corpse fetish.

Necrophilia : Sexual intercourse with the dead.

Nymphomania : A morbid sexual desire in the female.

Oedipus Complex : Sexual desire of the son for his mother, with hostility to the father.

Oralism : Sexual pleasure obtained through the use of the mouth on the sexual organs.

Pederasty (Sodomy): Insertion of the penis in the anus for the purpose of sexual gratification. This term is used for the practice of the act of sodomy upon children by adults.

Pedophilia : The condition in which a child or adolescent is chosen as the sexual object.

Perversion : The deviation of the sexual impulse from its normal goal.

Pervert : One who indulges in unnatural sexual acts or fantacies.

Piquers : Sexual sadists who stab their victims usually girls or women, with sharp instruments.

From 'CRIME and the SEXUAL PSYCHPATH' (op. cit)

All men and women have some sex perversions—but, mostly they are known to them and in some cases to a few others. Everyone is sexually decent until he is caught for sex perversions. When caught, everyone—including the sex-perverts-looks at him/her with contempt and aversion. WHY?

452

If filthy expressions and foul language are considered as symptoms of recidivism, then many police officers will be recidivists.

453

Attitude to crimes and frequency of occurrence of such crimes may be taken to decide the seriousness of recidivism. What is the attitude of police officers to the employment of third degree methods and use of vulgar language? Decide it before calling an individual to be a recidivist.

454

There is a feeling that poverty leads to crimes. This view is not emperically proved. But, there is another view that affluence leads to crime and the view is proved. There is yet another view that too much of affluence and money leads to too much of crimes of all descriptions Right?

455

Corruption leads to corruption and crimes. Corruption and power lead to henious crimes and recidivism.

456

Sub-culture of criminality in the society is found to be an explanation for persistence in criminal behaviour. Some studies and court judgements show that there exists a sub-culture of criminality in police stations. Is it because police stations are places where criminals are handled or is it because the policemen/officers therein express their criminal traits in a free way?

457

What is the nature of sub-culture seen in police stations? Is it a subculture of civility, decency, justness, fair-mindedness and honesty? Or is it a sub-culture of corruption, concoction, crookedness?

458

When the society itself is having a criminal culture or sub-culture, there may not be any meaning in saying that you are a criminal or you are not a criminal. Suffice to say what type of crime a person commits and how he manages it. The question of 'why' does not arise!

459

There exist many sub-cultures of criminality in the dominant culture that is seen in this great country of ours. The politicians' sub-culture—the businessmens' sub-culture and the bureaucrats' sub-culture. There is, no doubt, the criminalization of politics and there are criminals in politics, business and bureaucracy. Compared to those in such area, who is after all a petty thief, a pick-pocket or a small scale gambler?

460

Crimes may become a way of life for some. The liquor lobby who manufacture various brands spuriously or illegally live in crimes. They humour the law-enforcement officers and they consider corruption as an investment to their business. A lot of status and prestige may be given to such criminals and crime-racketeers.

461

Criminality is the expression of criminality or near criminality in the society.

462

Some research studies show that there are criminal lawyers as well as lawyer criminals. Likewise, there are criminal police officers as well as police officer criminals. Like knows the like—this is a Latin proverb and therefore, there is a nexus among the criminals, lawyer criminals and police officer criminals. Is it true?

463

A criminal can feel comfortable in committing crimes only if and if only there exists a situation wherein his criminal behaviour has become customary. Many criminals who are involved in crime—syndicates, adulteration, sale of spurious liquor, corruption-mafia, share-scam etc. feel quite comfortable to lead a pleasant life. At the same time, ordinary people involved in blue-collar crimes and no collar crimes do not feel comfortable. Why?

464

The society does not accept blue collar or no collar crimes. There is the society's reaction to the murder, rape, forgery, theft etc. and the reaction is still vindictive and retributive. At the same time, the same society tolerates "high collar" crimes and such crimes include 'share-scams, fake companies, commission-rackets, high level corruption etc. In many ways, the society encourages such top collar crimes.

465

The support and encouragement given by corrupt law-enforcement officers are found to be another explanation for recidivism. Corruption is not an "one-time business"–it is a continuous affair. Crime-syndicates, gambling, smuggling, manufacture and sale of illict liquor etc. can be done only with the knowledge, encouragement and approval of the law enforcement officers. It means that recidivism survives only with the support of recidivists.

466

If higher recidivists support high level recidivism, then lower level recidivists support low level recidivism. Instances are there to show that the constables/head constables encouraging pickpockets, burglars and thieves to commit crimes (repeat crimes) on condition that a share of the booty goes to them.

467

How to reform the "law enforcement recidivists"?—appears to be more difficult than reforming the recidivists who commit traditional crimes. In an age of recidivism, it is perhaps only through recidivism that the wisdom can rule.

468

Atonement, expiation, feeling of remorse, meditation, guilt-feeling etc. are found to be absent in a recidivist's life. He

SEX-CRIMES : DICTIONARY

--4

Psycho-Sexual Infantilism	:	A condition in which a chronologically adult individual remains sexually fixed at an infantile stage.
Pygmalionism	:	The sexual desire for a statue : A statue-fetish.
Sadism	:	(Algolagnia) A pervertion in which the libido becomes misdirected or perverted, so that the act of inflicting pain becomes in itself an object of sexual gratification.
Sapphism	:	Titillation of the clitoris through mutual masturbation or cunnilingus practised by females.
Satyriasis	:	Excessive venereal impulse in the male.
Scoptophilia	:	Synonymous with voyeurism.
Sodomy	:	Anal copulation
Transvestitism	:	Sexual pervertion characterised by the wearing of the clothes of opposite sex, and the desire to assume the name and role of the opposite sex.
Tribady	:	Intimate homosexual relationship between females (lesbians), the active individual assumes the male character towards the female partner in the sexual acts.
Triolism	:	A form of exhibitionism in which the subject desires to perform the sexual act with several partners or in the presence of several persons.
Uranism	:	A condition of homosexuality.
Urnids	:	Female homosexuals
Urnings	:	Male homosexuals
Urolagnia	:	A condition found in sado-masochism and fetishism in which the person is sexually aroused through the sight and odour of urine.
Urophilia	:	A psychopathic condition in which the individual has a fetish for urine.
Viraginity	:	A condition found in female homosexuals analogous to the effeminate in males.
Voyeurism	:	The desire to see or to be a witness to sexual practices.
Zoophilia	:	A passion for animals, often fetishistic in nature; erotic sexual relationship with animals.

From 'CRIME and the SEXUAL PSYCHOPATH'
by J. Paul De River

considers everything as his success and what more? He feels proud of himself. What about law enforcement recidivism? The law enforcement officers who are recidivists in corruption, use of third-degree methods, concoction of evidence, manipulation of records too do not have atonement, expiation, feeling of guilt etc.

469

'Truth backed by law, procedure and evidence'—This seems to be the philosophy of some police officers. Firstly, they ask: "What is the truth?" and they understand the truth. Secondly, they find out a law to book the crime-doer. They adopt the procedures and concoct evidence to see that the truth is brought out. In other words, the end justifies the means and that is all about their law enforcement!

470

Moralizing the misdeeds, rationalizing the misdoings, inducing the younger generation to do illegal things for a noble purpose during law enforcement etc. seem to be the oft-resorted strategies to administer 'justice'. Sofar, the approach could not yield good results and so forth no one hopes that it will.

471

'Attention to the crimes and not to the crime-doers'? The approach is found to be always better. But, can the police resort to it? Yes, why not?

472

'Enforcing the laws or abiding by laws'—Which is more difficult ? The former is easier and calls for fairness and justness. Abiding by law is easier, for it requires only willingness and desire to do so.

473

Denying justice and delaying justice—both are crimes. Hurrying justice and burying justice--both are also crimes.

474

Beware of pick-pockets, politicians, preachers, pleaders,

policemen, priests and please-men. All of them carry on their work with, a 'mens rea' to pick-pocket others' money!

475

A man without a criminal mind can not survive in the world. For, he has to live among criminals of all descriptions. Hence, if he is not a criminal, he is an exception to humanity.

476

Every individual has the potency to become a crime-doer. But, there is no need that he should be caught always and everytime he commits crimes. Hence, he continues to be a law abiding man until he is proved otherwise.

477

A crime is equal to 1000 words against the police and a detection of the same is equal to 10000 words in favour of police.

478

It is not the actual detection of crimes the police hope to make—but some detections today and now make the police efficient and effective. Never fool the people by a media-wash showing that the criminal will be soon caught when the fact is otherwise. The police can not fool the people always and every time.

479

If there is any one secret of successful police investigation, it lies in the ability of the investigator to get the crime-doer's point of view and appreciate things from his angle as well as from the police angle.

480

Understand a criminal does not mean stand under a criminal or make the criminal to stand under the police investigator. Never be succeptible to corruption or to coercion.

481

Listening to a suspect's version is 95 per cent of police interrogation, taking necessary action to varify what he says makes another 3 per cent and the remaining 2 per cent is nothing but following up with him to ensure his satisfaction in police work. The suspect has a right to be happy when he is under police custody.

482

Evaluate a lost case-not by initiating disciplinary action against the investigator but by deeper analysis and penetrating insights in to the causes of acquittals in police cases. There is a greater nobility in the nobility of doing noble things.

483

No police investigator ever tells that he lost a case in the court because of his faults. No accused ever tells that he got success in the court because of his faults. Both have merits and both claim to be meritorious.

484

Might is might and right is right, but no one wins if he is not prepared to fight. Criminal cases are acquitted and in every such acquittal, the accused wins over the might of the police. There, the right becomes the might.

485

Studies show that in fully two-thirds of the cases of wilful homicide, and aggravated assault, the culprits and the victims are known to each other; very often they are members of the same family and locality. Estimates of rape show further that in, perhaps, half the cases, the culprit and the victim are acquainted (U C R estimates).

486

Eve-teasing is a crime. So is the killing of the seducer of a woman. Bribery is a crime and so is the day-light robbery by terrorists. Misappropriation of government funds by high level bureaucrats is a crime and so does an affray in a public place. How can one put all these crimes together for the purpose of classification and analysis? It will be like lumping together common cold and lung cancer along with diarrhea and 'Aids.' For understanding the cause of each crime, for preventing each type, for suggesting remedies or reliefs etc., each category of crimes should be studied separately and meticulously.

DELINQUENT
TENDENCIES
WHY?
WHY?
WHY?
SMOKING IS INJURIOUS TO HEALTH.
YET, SOME CHILDREN SMOKE.....
BEEDI, CIGARETTE, GANJA

487

Arrest, interrogation, remand, trial, prosecution, incarceration, probation etc. are likely to have different effects and impacts on individual criminals. 'What is an arrest after all?'—asks the recidivist. 'O.K., you remand me'—says the hardened criminal. 'Incarceration?—well, this is my seventh conviction'—says the pick pocket. 'Interrogation?—What will my followers think about me'—asks the politician. 'My God, prosecution'—exclaims the first offender. And, all of them are mere procedures in justice administration-nothing more and nothing less.

488

What is the yardstick to question a hardened criminal? –a professional criminal? –a first offender? –a female offender? a murderer? –a terrorist? –a mafia criminal? Using the same yardstick is inappropriate, yet the police do everything in the same way.

489

The hands that arrest the crime-doers are handcuffered for causing rapes in custody, custodial violence, murder in lock-ups, wrongful confinement etc. There are directors general of police who are remanded, questioned, jailed for committing crimes which range from outraging the modesty of a woman to involving themselves in espionage cases. The question is who is a real criminal?

490

The police, prosecutor, press, defence, judge and correction—all these agencies work together or should work together for achieving highest happiness, protection and safety for the people. All sub-systems in justice administration work with public fund. Nevertheless, what is seen today is a fight among the various agencies. Each agency is alleged to involve itself in competing efficiently with one another.

491

Criminality, when taken out of police personality, will show a service sought after everywhere by people. A research estimate shows that the police are better than many other services under government.

492

There is no information as to how many thefts take place amidst us. There is no information as to how much tax evation, bribery, corruption and other forms of thievery from the public take place. Anyway, one thing is certain—i.e., the economic losses caused just by one tax evasion or corruption will be far greater than those caused by all the offences conventionally considered as offences under the Indian Penal Code 1860.

493

Price-rigging has a corrosive effect on the moral standards by which Indian business is conducted. The businessmen defraud their customers. Bribery is a cancer in Indian social life. The government employees expoit their official position to the advantage of those who offer illegal gratification. Corruption is a way of life for many politicians and top level bureaucrats and it has a threatening effect on the financial stability and economic growth of the Country. In the background of all these syndicate—while collar—political—bureaucratic—business—economic—social crimes, what is after all a simple theft?, a simple hurt?, a simple trespass? The policemen are found to be still sleepless about these small scale offences committed by ordinary mortals!!

494

Prostitution, drug-addiction, alcoholism, bribery, corruption, pilfering of government funds by the bureaucrats/political higher ups and offences of like nature are not only numerous, but they present to ordinary policemen with problems they are ill-equipped to solve. What to do?

495

Misuse of authority or exercise of pseudo authority by policemen/officers are crimes in every sense. They are distasteful to many, but how many people in the society will raise their voice against these oft-ractised illegal police actions?

496

Petty offenders occupy much of the time of most of the policemen. Not only that, they clog the lower courts and crowd the prisons all over the Country. Nobody knows the purpose of imprisonment for many of these petty offenders!

497

Why does crime increase in the society? An immediate answer to the question is that there is population increase. Yes, there is. Another answer is that there is better reporting of crimes. Yes, there is. Are there any other causes for the increase in crimes? Yes, there are. And to learn them, there should be a Research and Analysis Wing in every police department and we do not find any such units seriously functioning in any police organization in India.

498

Crimes committed by police are more exposed to the public by the media—often more than the crimes committed by the people. The impact is that there is a growing feeling among the people that there are more criminals in police department than what they are in the general public.

499

Many police officers think that individuals are responsible for the commission of crimes and they operate on that assumption. Ofcourse, the police can deal with individual offenders, but they have not designed or devised anything by which the conditions which breed crimes in society are eliminated.

500

No police organization, however well staffed and efficiently administered, will or can rid a society of crime if the people are not prepared to prevent crimes—if the conditions prevailing in the society are conducive for the commission of crimes.

501

The crime-doer goes via a continuum from police to prosecutor—to court to correctional institution—to the society. But, one doubts very much whether or not there is proper

PRISON OFFICIALS' THOUGHTS

I AM THE KING OF ROME AND ABOVE GRAMMER

MANY PRISON OFFICIALS BEHAVE LIKE KINGS IN THEIR KINGDOMS WHEREIN EACH INMATE IS ONLY A SUBJECT

co-ordination among the various sub-systems in justice administration. The modern thinking is that there should be real co-ordination and cooperation among the various agencies involved in justice administration to achieve the objective—i.e., the correction and rehabilitation of the criminal.

502

The police is a sub-system that investigates a crime–the prosecution is a sub-system which argues that the accused is guilty—the defence is a sub-system that pleads not guilty—the court is a sub-system that adjudicates—and the correctional agency is a sub-system which sees that the offender is removed from society and corrected—the society is a sub-system which aids all the sub-systems to function properly. Hence, there should be proper co-ordination and cooperation among them.

503

What is called 'victim-precipitation?' It means: "in a particular situation, the behaviour of the victim is interpreted by the offender as a direct invitation to commit the crime on him (Cf. Amir). This means the victim has had something positively to do with his or her own victimization.

504

"Some of the victims are in a real sense instigators. Their attitudes, wishes and personalities seem to provoke action by the doer....." (Hans Von Hentig). Here, one may see victim precipitation.

505

"Attitudes of submitting, conniving, passively submitting, co-operative, contributory, provocative, instigative, soliciting" (Hentig) etc. are indicators or signals of victim precipitation.

506

There are instances in which one may observe a full and total participation by the victim and it is called 'victim participation'. In alleged rape-cases, the victim participation becomes an important point to be decided.

507

"If a person has not acted with reasonable self-protective behaviour in handling his money, jwellery or other valuables and has become the victim of robbery, he can not be considered as an innocent victim". He has surely created a "temptation—opportunity" situation-giving the criminal an invitation, provocation, incentive and help (Fooner).

508

Victim-compensation is an internationally accepted concept now. India too has accepted it and the courts now award compensation to the victims of crime. A law on victim-compensation is under preparation now. Victim compensation is also awarded to the victims of police torture and harassment.

509

Equal Justice System is now favoured more than the criminal justice or victim justice system. The Equal Justice System ensures justice to the crime-doers and to the victims of offence alike. Hence, the system is called Crimino-Victim Justice System.

510

Human Rights Conventions—especially the Convention Against Torture — say that laws should be enacted to ensure adequate compensation to victims of custodial torture — murder - rape - or harassment. The National Human Rights Commission now inquires into all cases of torture in police custody and awards compensation.

511

Criminals are criminals — victims are victims — the police are police. All of them have specific roles to play for the betterment of society. Society progresses and moves forward to an Omega — a Cosmic Power and every one contributes his share for achieving the objectives.

CHAPTER - 5

CRIME AND CORRECTION : IS PREVENTION OF CRIME POSSIBLE?

512

Women offenders detected by police are few and handled by the police are fewer when compared with men-offenders. Yet, accusations against police for mishandling of women are indeed very severe. Why ? The accusations may not be altogether baseless and hence, be careful. Do everything as per law and in accordance to the procedure established by law.

513

Why are there only few women offenders in all societies ?—in all cultures ?—at all times? One reason for it may be lack of opportunities for women to crime-producing situations and another is the difference in cultural training. One may admit that there exists greater leniency on the part of police towards crimes committed by women. Unless a crime committed by a woman is not that serious to call for immediate police action, usually, it is leniently viewed.

514

Stability of social order is surely a controlling factor in the commission of crimes of certain categories such as offences against public peace, tranquility, human body etc. Establishment of a stable social order may therefore help the police to control and prevent crimes.

515

Rural areas show lower incidences of crimes than urban areas. Hence, police vigilance should be more in urban areas to

'STRIKE WHILE THE IRON IS HOT"

PAROLE TO INMATES IN PRISONS

PAROLE SHOULD BE GRANTED AT THE APPROPRIATE TIME–AND THE APPROPRIATE TIME IS THE BEST TIME WHEN AN INMATE SHOULD BE RELEASED. ANY LONGER STAY HAS DISADVANTAGES FOR REFORMATION control crime. Rural societies are more stable, isolated and homogeneous than urban societies.

516

Studies show that the highest rates of crime and delinquency are found in the physically deteriorated and disorganised areas in and around the centre of the cities. The migration, disorganisation, dislocation of population, mobility, slum areas, urban culture, anonymity in city life etc. are found to indirectly encourage criminality by increasing opportunities to commit law violations.

517

Personality inventories and clinical observations indicate that the crime-doers and criminals handled by police are somewhat more neurotic than the police officers/men themselves, but the differences are not very much or marked. The types of neuroses observed in offenders are similar to those seen in police officers/men and the general public.

518

Individuals possessing average or superior intelligence who are neither neurotic nor psychotic, but, at the same time, are social misfits and borderline mental cases are labelled psychopathic personalities—says Page. He continus: "This is a general psychiatric category that includes pathological liars, sexual perverts, tramps, amoral individuals, misanthropes, eccentrics and certain types of emotionally unstable individuals". Psychopaths are seen both among law enforcement officers and among the members of the general public.

519

Do the police officers experience guilt feelings when they mishandle or manhandle a suspect in a crime. If they do not have, they are called psychopaths in that area. Some police officers try to justify their otherwise illegal acts to crime-doers and suspects. This is an indication of their guilt feelings and to that extent, they are not psychopaths.

520

Today's juvenile delinquents are tomorrow's adult criminals. This need not be true. Studies show that most of the juvenile delinquents do not become adult criminals and likewise, most of the adult criminals have no history of juvenile delinquency. Hence, there is no need to deal with a juvenile delinqents with any pre-conceived theory that they are going to be adult criminals tomorrow.

521

In every society, there will be some laws to regulate the social life of the people. With the passage of time, these laws become antiquated and fail to regulate the life of the people. In the Indian Penal Code, there are many sections which are of no use today. The police use only a few among them to register criminal cases, others have become meaningless in the changed social conditions.

522

As time passes by, there may take place changes in the values and thinking of the people. Accordingly, the laws have to be changed. The Indian Penal Code came into existence in 1860, i.e., nearly one and half of a century ago. It came at a different socio-political melieu and it is not very relevant today. Yet, the police in India try to implement the laws. They fail to understand that many of the crimes committed by people today are not defined in the Indian Penal Code, 1860.

523

Most successful crimes today are not detected by police and today many reported crimes remain unsolved by the police. What to do?

524

There are numerous laws in the Country and there are numerous ways by which a person can commit crimes. And there are numerous ways by which the police can make a person to be a criminal.

525

Crime-doers and victims of crimes are people of all castes, sub-castes, ages, incomes, status and backgrounds.

526

The causes of crime are many and their cures are more speculative and contraversial. What can the police do to find out the causes of crime and their cures ?

527

The most successful crime is surely a secret crime.

528

All crimes, wherever they are committed, are committed by human beings. All crimes, wherever they are investigated are investigated by people—the police—who have almost all characteristics of the criminals themselves.

529

No police services, however effectively they work, can rid a society of crime if there is not a widespread ethical motivation.

530

Can the police curb crimes—by changing the penal laws? or adding new laws? or adopting new legal procedures?

531

Can the problem of crime be solved by efficient police work—by imposing very severe penalty?—by correcting and reforming criminals ?

532

Some criminologists and police officers are inclined to think crime as a form of social alienation.

533

Detection of crime, apprehension of the criminal, prosecution of the offender, trial of the offence and then punishment—and then what ?

HUMAN RIGHTS AND PRISONS

Overcrowded prisons, prolonged detention of undertrial prisoners, unsatisfactory living conditions, lack of treatment programmes and allegations of an indifferent and even inhuman approach of prison staff have repeatedly attracted the attention of critics over the years......

The Prison Act was largely based on deterrent principles concerned more with prison management than with the treatment of prisoners and gave more consideration to prison offences and punishment than to their effect......

Protection of society as an objective of punishment has been universally accepted and this can be achieved through reformation and rehabilitation of the offenders.....

Cf. Human Rights Behind The Prison Wall
by T. Ananthachari.

534

Is crime a disease and the crime-doer a patient ? If so, the detection, apprehension, prosecution, trial etc. should be done to treat the troubled patient—the troubled society.

535

How to punish a crime-doer ? Take into account the seriouness of his offence?—or—by taking into account the result of the diagnosis of his need for correction. The question is: "how to handle the offender before the sentencing ?

536

'Crime and correction' is an 'input-output system.' That is to say—from the hands of the police to the prosecutor and from there to the jurisdiction of the court—to incarceration behind the bars and then back to the society. The out-put is and should be a reformed citizen. But, the inefficiency, the failure, the fall-out of the objective during the 'input-output' process are indeed very notorious.

537

Do the police employ third-degree methods of investigation when they interrogate suspects in a crime ? The answer is 'yes'. If so why do the police use them ? Their answer is: "We use third degree methods, because the suspects deserve them". The approach is no doubt retributive in nature. The police need more information about crime, criminals, correction etc. and their role in the justice system.

538

Remember, remember and remember always that a detinue in police custody or a suspect under interrogation retain all the basic rights enjoyed by the free citizens, except those which are taken away as a result of his being a detinue or a suspect.

539

Detention in a police lock-up does not and can not render an individual a non-entity. He is a person and a person with inherent dignity. He enjoys many rights and his rights are not subjected or surrendered to the whims of police authorities.

540

A suspect in police custody is a weak person. A police officer in the company of other police officers in a police station is a strong person. In such situations, he has surcharged energy. There may not come any human sympathy or consideration unless human beings in police stations decide to be so. "A criminal after-all" attitude is often taken and it continues to dominate the police mind during interrogation and detention.

541

Police everywhere in the world behave alike to the suspects and detainees. There is no difference in kind as the difference is only in degrees as far as police behaviour to the suspect/detained (or vice versa) is concerned. See the American law: "No law enforcement officer shall attempt to induce an arrested person to make a statement, or otherwise to cooperate, by subjecting, or threatening to subject, such person or any person in whom such person is interested by any form of abuse, including any practice designed to unsettle, frighten or degrade, or by depriving any arrested person of adequate food, water, medical attention, rest or other physical necessities".

542

Supreme Court has given directions for issuing custody memo to the people whom the police want to take into custody. Some police officers think that the directives of the Court are likely to cause delay in police work in many ways. The fear is baseless. See the American law: "If a law enforcement officer stops any person who he suspects or has reasonable cause to suspect may have committed a crime, the officer shall warn such person as promply as is reasonable under the circumstances, and in any case before engaging in any sustained questioning--

(i) that such person is not obliged to say anything, and anything he says may be used as evidence against him.

(ii) that within twenty minutes, he will be released unless he is arrested;

(iii) that if he is arrested, he will be taken to a police station where he may promptly communicate by telephone with counsel, relatives or friends and

(iv) that he will not be questioned unless he wishes, and that if he wishes to consult a lawyer or have a lawyer present during questioning, he will not be questioned at this time, and that after being taken to the station-house a lawyer will be furnished to him prior to questioning if he is unable to obtain one".

543

A crime-doer is an individual and he is infront of the police—a mammoth agency with heavy manpower and resources. The suspect is helpless and therefore his interest should be protected. Hence, no police officer should make attempts to induce an arrested person to make a statement or otherwise cooperate by —

(1) questioning of such unfair frequency, length or persistence as to constitute harassment to such person; or

(2) any other method, which, in light of such person's age, intelligence and mental and physical condition, unfairly undermines his ability to make a choice whether to make a statement or otherwise cooperate (American law).

544

Lie detection or polygraph tests are being administered to suspects more frequently than what they were earlier. The law for administering such test is not very clear in India. Nevertheless, the law well settled in the west is: "No law enforcement officer shall seek to obtain information from an arrested person by using drugs or hypnosis, or a polygraph test or other such procedure designed to determine the truthfulness of statements by body reactions, unless, after such procedure has been proposed, such person has had an opportunity to consult with counsel for a period adequate to obtain advice concerning such procedure and has consented thereto" (American law).

545

Some police officers in India think that the people in developed countries are also developed and so do the police officers. Therefore, they subscribe to the view that the attitudes of police to the suspects (vice versa) too are well developed. This is not a true proposition as the police and people are alike in all countries and in every culture. If at all the proposition is true, there is no justification in resorting to ruthless methods merely because the suspects come from a developing or undeveloped country.

546

Any attempt to induce an arrested person to make a statement by indicating that such person is legally bound to do so is a deception in police procedure. Never resort to such unethical and illegal practices.

547

Who is a criminal ? A person may be considered as a criminal only if and if only he himself regards him as one who has violated the criminal law of the Country. So far, a person is regarded as a criminal if he is caught by the police as one who has violated the criminal law. There are instances of false cases registered against innocent people. Surely one can not be a criminal if he is caught by the police. A person is regarded as a criminal if he is regarded so by the society. A person is said to be a criminal if he is regarded to be so by himself, by the police, by the court and by the society at large.

548

Legal definition of a criminal is no definition at all—i.e., a person is said to be a criminal if and only when he is convicted by a court of law—for, there are instances of innocent people convicted by the courts of law and guilty people escaping punishment.

549

The police departments always claim that they enforce all the laws equally, but, one may surely see that they enforce laws only selectively. There are statutes which the department does not attend at all. And there is differential application of laws to different individuals. As a result, many law violators do not come to police attention and action.

550

How do the people who violate the law come to police

attention ? Studies conduced by the author show that 92 per cent of the crimes committed by people are reported to the police and they are reported by the people themselves. Police come to respond to law violations only when they are informed about them. Police themselves find out law violations only in 2% of the cases. The rest are somehow reach the police.

551

What is police corruption ? A police officer is said to be corrupt if he receives money—either in cash or in kind—for doing a thing which he is otherwise bound to do-like granting bail, behaving decently, avoiding humiliation, providing food etc.—or not to do something which he is not legally authorized to do or to exercise a legitimate descretion for improper purposes.

552

"Rotten eggs" theory of corruption—i.e., it is only a few individuals in police department are corrupt and the rest are not corrupt-may be a good explanation to explain away the problem or to mitigate the seriousness of the issue. The theory never explains the causes and cures of corruption in police department.

553

"Low visibility" of police work—"the secret community" character of police organization—the authority to use their discretions in anyway they want—the exercise of pseudo-authority—the hierarchical tolerarance of corrupt practices—the sharing of corruption money by all in a unit—helplessness of the people to get things done without offering corruption money and many more factors can be the causes of corruption in police department.

554

Police has got only 11th rank in the corruption graph-says one study. Police, has 4th rank in the corruption graph-says another study. No one wants to dispute about the validity of these study results, yet every-body knows that there is corruption in police department. Why to have a debate on the extent and intensity of corruption ?

ORGANISED CRIMINALITY

THE INVISIBLE BOSS
OF CRIME SYNDICATES

THE REAL CRIMINAL

BEHIND

MANY ORGANISED
—MAFIA—CRIMES ARE INVISIBLE
TO MANY

555

Some police officers regard violence—roughing up—as particularly effective in handling of such cases as property offences, where confessions from the suspects are difficult to be obtained—as particularly necessary in handling of such cases as sex offences, where convictions from the courts are not easily possible. They also argue that the people approve of such police torture on property offenders and sex offenders. It works as deterrent to potential criminals. Arguments are weighty and worth nothing. But, it may be remembered that the officer who employs torture on the offenders should be prepared to suffer the consequences of his action if matters go beyond his control. Morality is one thing and legality is quite another thing in many instances.

556

Do the suspected— the arrested— the prosecuted—the accused—the convicted—get justice of any kind ? A criminologist answers this question in the negative. According to him, a suspected is processed through the bureaucratic machinery with little or no concern for his rights—inherent rights and Constitutional rights. Is this view correct ?

557

Bureaucratic coverage for the crimes the members of the bureaucracy commit is indeed shocking. The bureaucratic coverage can produce a variety of criminalogical responses including corruption, concoction, manipulation, misappropriation etc. The bureaucratic system prevailing in any society protects the corrupt, exploitative, illegal and unfair interests of the bureaucratic community.

558

The very nature of the bureaucratic-economic-system encourages egoism, exploitation, misuse of authority and miscarriage of justice—i.e., for the achievement of the unrestricted pursuit of self-interest and financial growth for the bureaucrats. For this, they may do anything including the formation of a nexus with corrupt people in society.

559

Any injustice done to an individual by the bureaucracy can be covered by the bureaucracy if that needs be. "After all it was done by a brother in bureuacracy"—seems to be the attitude of government servants. Hence, justification and rationalization of the ill-doings committed by the bureaucratic brethren become the order of the day. The organization of the bureaucratic brethren community commits a variety of crimes against the unorganised people in society. The activities are criminal.

560

Police is an organised community and they can do a lot of things against individuals who are the members of an unorganised community. Use of third degree methods, violence against individuals, concoction of evidence etc. may be owing to the police advantage over the unorganised people in society.

561

When a crime is committed by an individual in the unorganised people's society, the police can register a case and investigate it. But, when a member of the organised police community commits a crime, then also the police registers a case and investigates it. There are criticisms about this approach—that the people have no trust in police registration and investigation of crimes committed by them.

562

Reactions to crimes committed by police take different forms. Some kinds of crimes—calling filthy names to people—are rarely reacted against. Some other kinds of crime—beating a person in public or police custody without causing visible injury—are sparingly reacted against. A few crimes—custodial violence, torture etc.—are reacted against with fear and reluctance. All crimes—murder in police custody, custodial rape etc.—are invariably reacted against by public agitations. This means that it is only very serious and heinous crimes committed by the police are resented and reacted against.

563

People do not react vehemently to many crimes committed

by police, not because they do not want to react against but because they are afraid of the police reactions against the people who react to police crimes. People's inability, fear or weakness to react against police crimes should not be confused as their approval of police actions and activities.

564

Communal forces, labour forces, student forces, political forces—and thus the organised forces—can afford to commit crimes with some immunity. Likewise, the police forces also can commit crimes with some immunity—say research studies. People who commit crimes are often individuals and as such they can not claim immunity for the acts they do just like people in organised groups enjoy. One and the same act committed by a person individually and by a person being a member of the organised group is viewed differently. Correspondingly, crimes become no crimes when they are committed by organised groups.

565

An act is interpreted as a crime by the law enforcement officers. A simple hurt can be interpreted as an act of voluntarily causing hurt or even an attempt to murder. Punishments to the crime vary depending upon the interpretation that is given to the act. 'Beauty lies in the beholder's eye'—this principle applied in the interpretation of crimes takes away the objectivity in identifying and analysing crimes.

566

Some ill-informed 'crime-doers' are persuaded to plead guilty in courts. They are made to believe that the courts may take a lenient view in such situations. The 'crime-doers' believe everything they are told and get convicted. This strategy is called the bureaucratically ordained and controlled short-cuts. It is nothing but miscarriage of justice and outright violations of the accused's rights in the system of justice administration.

567

A society without crimes has never existed—and—will never exist. Likewise, an individual can not live without violating the laws—and—will never live without violating the laws. If there is any one who does not violate the laws, he is either dead or not yet born.

568

Think always that there is a better way to do things—even to commit crimes—say organised criminals. Many criminals caught by the police always think: "There was a better way to execute the crime, but failed".

569

Police officers are still concerned with the legal aspects of crime. Their concern is more object-centred and act-centred. There is yet another view and that is—the crime should be viewed as person-centred and the person should be corrected.

570

"My crimes are my unique choice and nobody can claim the credit for my crimes "— I thought in this way once, but later I understood that the crimes could not merely be an individualistic affair. Every crime has its social impacts and dimensions.

571

One's understanding of crimes depends upon what he thinks about the laws and their necessity in society. Until he really understands the necessity of laws, he will not and can not understand crimes and criminal behaviours.

572

Man has limitless capacity to love oneself selfishly and enormous capacity to love others. The human history is a history of violence to one's selfishness on one side or on one's love for others on the other side. In both instances, there is the unfailing expressions of man's violence prone-psyche.

573

Violence in police custody is no news anywhere"......... Battered spinal cords, crushed heads, mangled limbs and pulverised testicles litter the findings of reports on the death" (P. Chawla) in police custody.

574

When a person is arrested, he is granted bail by the police. If he is not granted bail, he is produced before the court. The court may grant bail or remand him to police custody or to judicial custody. What is judicial custody in India ? It is the custody in jail under a judicial order. Jail is a jail and custody in jails can not be called judicial custody. Custody in jails under a judicial order can not be called 'judicial custody'. In the event of acquittal, those who go to jails under judicial custody are found to have suffered incarceration without being guilty of any crime. What an injustice indeed!

575

How many suspects who are refused bail are acquitted after the trial ? No reliable data is available on the issue. Yet it may be stated that over 20 per cent of the remanded to judicial/police custody are not convicted. What justification is there for the "justice system" to subject people into a sort of penal custody with penal food and penal treatment even when the crimes against them are not proved ? Is it not miscarriage justice ?

576

Of the people remanded to police custody or judicial custody prior to the trial,—i.e., the jailed defendants—how many are able to defend their cases properly in the courts ? My own studies show that they are more likely to be convicted than bailed defendants. Being jailed defendants, what can they do ? Is it not miscarriage of justice ?

577

A jailed defendant is likely to get more severe punishment than a bailed defendant. One reason is that he may not get easy access to lawyers or if at all the has access to lawyers through somebody else, who is there to spend money to a lucrative legal advice ?

578

How many people granted bail on their "own recognizance" will escape and see that they do not appear in courts ? No studies have been conducted in India to know the impact of

CRIME IS LEARNT

Criminal behaviour is learnt. It is learnt in interaction with other persons in a process of communication. The communication can be often verbal and at times through gestures. The principal part of learning of criminal behaviour occurs within intimate personal groups. And when criminal behaviour is learnt, the learning includes:

i. Techniques of committing crimes
ii. Specific directions of motives, drives, rationalization and attitudes. The specific direction of motives and drives is learnt from definitions of legal codes as favourable or unfavourable.
iii. A person becomes delinquent because of an excess of definitions favourable to the violation of laws
iv. The process of learning criminal behaviour by association with criminal and anticriminal patterns involves all of the mechanisms that are involved in any other learning. Cf. EDWIN H. SUTHERLAND.

such a practice. Nevertheless, studies conducted elsewhere show that only negligible number of people who are granted release on their "own recognizance" fail to appear to courts. In one study in U.S.A., it was seen that only three out of the 275 persons thus released did not appear in the court. Criminologists view that the refusal to grant bail or granding bail only on furnishing of huge amounts are not necessary for administration of justice.

579

Between the bonded defendants and nonbonded defendants—i.e., those who are released on "own recognizance" and those who are released on the assurance of a bail bondsman—who is better to keep up their promise to the court ? Studies show that there is no difference between the bonded and nonbonded defendants in their absconding nature. Only a very negligible number from both groups abscond themselves and the "bondedness" is not a deciding factor in their abscondings.

580

Crime in India is mainly the work of males and what is the reason for the disproportionate contribution of males to criminality ? This may be an old picture. Recently, more and more women are found involved in the commission of crimes—either alone or along with males. One interpretation of this changing trend—i.e., parity with men in terms of crimes—is that it reflects the growing social equality of women with men and the more open opportunities for women to involve themselves in criminal activities.

581

What is called "hidden criminality ?" Hidden criminality means the extent of unreported crimes or crimes committed, but not known (or reported to) to the authorities. No study is available in India on this, yet some studies conducted in America show that the group of offenders that comes to the attention of authorities represent only a segment of a large collection of criminals (Don C. Gibbons).

582

A person, once he is arrested or taken into custody, is processed through the bureaucratic machinery. Those who man and manage the bureaucratic machinery push the suspects/ arrested from one stage to another in the operation—until atlast the case is chargesheeted or referred to stating that the entire procedure took place as a result of "Mistake of Fact". Cases dropped or referred to because of "mistake of fact" are on the increase and everybody seems to think: "all is well that ends well". But the mistake done to individuals by the gigantic bureaucracy is indeed a 'miscarriage of justice" and he deserves compensation and the bureaucracy responsible should be proceeded against.

583

Though correction and rehabilition are accepted as the twin objectives of punishment, one sees that retribution and deterrence dominate the attitude and approach of the bureaucratic machinery. The theories of reformation, resocialization, behaviour modification or remaking of the law-breakers do not operate much during the pre-trial and trial proceedings. What is required is an attitudinal change in the sub-systems of justice administration.

584

The classical school of criminology considered a law-violator as a wilful hedonist. The school also believed that the criminals made deliberate decisions to be bad. The Indian Penal Code, the Criminal Procedure Code which came into existence during the latter part of the nineteenth century were influenced by the classical thoughts and therefore it was thought that the criminals could be deterred from criminality by police and judicious application of inflicting some pains on them. The same thinking dominates the attitude of police even now.

585

Being influenced by the classical thoughts, police stations were constructed without paying much attention to the correctional aspects. The lock-ups in police stations were the best examples to show that the law wanted retribution and deterrence to the crime-doers and potential criminals. The classical thoughts in a way gave birth to a behavioural pattern which was more oriented to infliction of pain and sufferings to the detained in police custody. Resultantly, the detained became victims of retribution and sufferers of pain while they were in police lock-ups. The same thinking dominates the police even now.

586

Human rights activists and people who advocate humanitarian approaches to the detained in police custody still find that the detained are dealt with in overly harsh ways by the police. They argue that humanitarianism to the suspects and the detained should dominate the police attitude and approaches to the detinues in police custody.

587

Humanitarian acts—such as providing sufficient food, allowing the detainees to wear clothes, permitting them to sleep etc—should not be considered as a leniency shown to the people in custody. Human handling of the detinues and humanitarian attitudes shown to them show fair treatment and just administration.

588

A person detained in police custody does not and can not behave in a normal way. The confinement in police lock-ups, the inconvenience therein, the deplorable conditions existing in the lock-ups, the attitude of the police personnel etc. will influence his behaviour. This is an abnormal situation and it will have its own impact upon the detinue. Understand him and adjust accordingly.

589

Suicidal deaths in lock-ups are on the increase and one reason for it is the influence of the environments in police lock-ups and outside on the detainees. Suicidal deaths can be reduced if the environments (influences) in police lock-ups are changed.

590

Miranda Rights followed in United States—i.e., the suspect has a right to counsel during police interrogation—may not be allowed in India. Yet the fact remains that the accused has a right to counsel is accepted as a sacred rights in all civilized

SUN GLASSES ?

JAUNDICE ?

A man who wants to see a crime in every human act does see it, for he wears sun-glasses which do not allow him to see objects as they are

Police are accused of seeing crimes and criminal intentions in every human act. They are blamed to be men affected by JAUNDICE and they see all things YELLOW — Is it true ?

countries. In U.S.A., the suspect has a right to remain silent. He has also a right to consult with his attorney. The police are law-bound to effectively advise the suspects of his rights. The suspects in India are also having many rights but they are not informed of them by the police before they are interrogated. Why ?

591

An interrogated in police custody is alone and there are many police officers/men. This 'state of being alone' in the police stations make a detainee in psychological tension. He is just a suspect and he has all the rights to see that his rights are respected and protected by the majority (police) community. Protecting the "minority's rights" is the duty of the "majority" in a democracy.

592

Crime is not a way of life for a law—breaker of the Indian Penal Code—1860 which enumerates traditional crimes like murder, rape, hurt, theft etc. It is a way of life for most of the businessmen, for many in politics, for some in bureauracy and for all in crime-syndicates.

593

Everyman in the society has a 'love—hate' relationship with crime and criminal acts. He enjoys the crimes committed and feels facinated by the portrayals of such commission of crimes in audio-visual media. At the same time, he hates them and never likes them to be committed against him.

594

Many police officers have a 'love—hate' relationship with crime and criminals. Many of them hate the crimes committed by the suspects in their custody and at the same time, love to commit crimes on the suspects to obtain a confession from them. Criminologists call this "love-hate" approach to be "dirting the law with dirty tactics".

595

"Violating the law against the violations of law"—is an example of love-hate relations to crime and criminals. Informal arrest (abduction of people by the law-enforcement officers), illegal detention (wrongful confinement in police custody), use of third degree methods, coercion, concoction, padding up of evidence etc. are examples of violating law (love crimes) and arrest, detention, investigation, prosecution of the case in a lawful manner for administering justice are examples of actions against law violations (hating crimes). Can the police violate the law to act against the violations of law ?

596

Every crime has an origin and development. No crime develops in a society all on a sudden—one day, too soon. For, the society can not accommodate too much of crimes. If a particular type of crime shows an abnormal increase, it is only a temporary phenomenon. It will have a natural death and will assume its natural growth in due course.

597

If the police do not do anything to check the growth of crime in society, what will be the impact? Don't worry. The society will develop its own strategies to check and control crimes—even without the assistance of police. Police are only an official agency to control crimes. There are many unofficial ways by which crimes are controlled.

598

Official control or unofficial control of crime—which is more important to check the growth of crimes ? Studies show that the unofficial methods of checking crimes is more effective to control crimes than the official strategies.

599

People do not commit crimes, because the people do not want to commit crimes. If somebody is determined to commit a crime, he commits it and the police can not control such commissions of crime. If at all the police are very active to control crimes, their activities have only temporary effects upon the commissions.

600

Police have many duties and crime control is one among their many duties. No police service can keep a continuous watch over the various categories of criminal activities in society.

601

If the police are very active and vigilant in controlling a particular type of crime in a particular area, the criminals who are determined to commit such crimes go away to another place where the police vigilance is least and they involve in the commission of crimes. If the police extend their vigilance to the new place, then the criminals go to yet another place to continue their criminal activities.

602

Prevention of crimes by police is more important than detection of crime. It is like saying: "prevention is better than cure". But, what type of crimes can the police prevent ? They can prevent a crime only if they know about it. But, the commission of many crimes are not known to police and therefore the questions. "What type of crimes can the police prevent or what type of crimes do the police prevent" ?

603

Some studies show that nearly 70 per cent of the crimes are committed within the family. Such crimes include domestic violence, disorderly conduct, harassment, menacing, reckless endangerment, assault, attempted assault between spouses or between parents and children, or between members of the same family or household. They also include suicides, family suicides, murder of family members, dowery deaths, burnings, burglary, consumption of alcohol etc. What can the police do to prevent crimes that take place in the family set-up or within the family ?

604

What role do the police have to settle family disorders ? They have no positive roles. The police should not think that the family problems are police problems. They also should not assume to themselves the responsibility to settling family issues which should be handled scientifically by professionally qualified experts in such matters.

MENTAL RETARDATION

Sub-types of mental retardation	I.Q. level
Mild retardation	50-70
Moderate retardation	35-49
Severe retardation	20-34
Profound retardation	Below 20

(D.S.M. III)

"Nothing is an offence which is done by a person who, at the time of doing it, by reason of unsoundness of mind, is incapable of knowing the nature of the act, or that, he is doing what is either wrong or contrary to law" (Cf. Section 84, Indian Penal Code-1860).

605

Sex crimes—such as rape, prostitution, adultery, homosexuality, beastiality etc.—are crimes which can not be usually prevented by police. What the police can do is to investigate such crimes if and when they are reported to them. Reporting of sex offences to police is not frequently resorted to as it is likely to cause more harm than good to the victims of rape. Conscientisation of sex-values is found to be a better strategy to control sex crimes than positive police action on such offences.

606

Drug-addiction, alcoholism, prostitution, sex-pervertions, family discords etc. are not police problems. They are the manifestations of psychiatric problems and they should be treated as such. Referral of such cases to appropriate treatment agencies is the best police strategy in such situations.

607

'Crimes in the street'—robberies, crude thefts, auto-thefts, extortion, assaults, affray, riots,—are special areas in which the police can extend their preventive strategies. Patrolling can surely help to reduce such crimes in the street at least for the time being.

608

Owing to the rapid growth in transport and communications, the news about crimes reach everywhere within no time. As a result, the people express their concern about law-breakings. At times, the police are helpless as their means of transportation and method of communication are of an inferior quality. Criminals may flourish and the police may cut a sorry figure.

609

Scientific study of the causation, detection, investigation, prosecution, trial and correction has never been an area of interest for the police. The police have been found to be interested only in detection and investigation. This policy of water-tight compartment of police studies about crimes and criminals make them to ignore the causative and preventive aspects of crime in society. A wholistic approach has been lacking for the treatment of crime and criminals in society.

610

Though criminology and correction are subjects for the police to study during their induction training courses, one wonders whether or not the subjects are taught by professionally qualified teachers. The result is that the subjects are not taught properly or if at all taught, it is not with a wholistic approach.

611

Every police officer thinks himself to be a crime-investigator. Perhaps, the existing laws make him to think so. The result is that everyone deals with crime and criminals in the way he likes. Many do not have any professional interest or if some have any interest, they are not exposed to the latest knowledge in the science of crime and criminals.

612

Crime is not at all inherent in human behaviour ? The police identify acts of one kind or another as criminal. For, a particular human behaviour to become criminal, somebody's conception of such an act must get accepted in the larger society and the society entrusts this work to the police. Hence the police officer/men should be well educated to use their discretion in the identification of human behaviour and criminal behaviour. One wonders whether or not the police today in India have education and wisdom to perform their job meaningfully.

613

Each criminal represents a legion of similar criminals in society. Epidemiology of crime and criminals should attract police interest to design and implement adequate police strategies to fight against crimes in society.

CHAPTER-6

CRIME AND CORRECTIONAL INSTITUTIONS : IS CORRECTION OF CRIME-DOERS ATTAINABLE?

614

'The doubting mind sees many ghosts'—This is a Chinese proverb. Likewise, a crime-doer sees everything alone by the police to be acts done against him and the policeman doubts everything a crime doer has done to be blame-worthy. Where is the meeting point of mutual suspicions? Both see ghosts in many situations.

615

'The cure is worse that the disease'—This is a proverb and many suspects in crime feel so as the treatments they receive in police stations and later during the stages of trial and jail are so horrible that they think that the cure is worse than the disease. Investigation, prosecution, trial and incarceration have and should have curative contents.

616

The worst animal on earth is the man—for, he only can be jealous, vindictive, atrocious, thankless etc. and he express such traits in his behaviour to other fellow beings.

617

Man has a mind and he alone can have mental disorders. Mental disorders can cause crimes and they can be affected to anyone on earth irrespective of his status, position, role, self-concept or ego-inflation.

PHOBIA

X, aged 62, farmer by occupation, was suffering from phobic ghosts. Just infront of his house, a 34 year old man met with an accident and died. Eversince, there was a talk in the village that his ghost walked around the area there threatening people. In fact, a woman, aged 26 was said to have been possessed by the ghost of the deceased.

X, the farmer was living with his old wife alone and was terribly afraid of the ghost. He used to hear the hauling of the ghost during night hours. During the dead of the night, he, at times, listened to strange sounds of the ghost beckoning him. He never went out of his room, even for urination during night hours without a stick. He thought that beating the ghost with a stick was very effective.

PHOBIC DISORDERS

Acrophobia	– Fear of high places
Algophobia	– Fear of pain
Astraphobia	– Fear of storms and thunder
Hematophobia	– Fear of blood
Mysophobia	– Fear of contamination of germs
Pyrophobia	– Fear of fire
Monophobia	– Fear of lonliness
Gynophobia	– Fear of women
Zoophobia	– Fear of animals
Ocholophobia	– Fear of crowds
Nyctophobia	– Fear of darkness
Claustophobia	– Fear of closed places
Agoraphobia	– Fear of open places
Pathophobia	– Fear of diseases
Syphilophobia	– Fear of syphilis

Besides, there may be phobia to toilet and bathrooms, to bugs, to cancer, to death, to light, to poisoning, to street, to vehicle, to landscape, to door knobs etc.

One day, he went outside his house for urinating at about 2 o'clock, when he found the ghost coming. He immediately took the stick and started to beat the ghost. The ghost in turn caught hold of the stick and returned the beatings. People gathered around and on detailed enquiry, it was found out that X was a ghost phobic and no police action was warranted against him.

(Cf. Human Behaviour and Law Enforcement)

618

'Nero was fiddling when Rome was on fire'—Let it not happen in a police station. Starving detinues should not be kept in hunger pangs when the officials enjoy sumptuous meals.

619

Never advise a crime-doer to make a confession of his guilt to a police officer. It is his statutory right to plead 'not guilty' even when he is 'guilty'. Legally guilty?—that is what is to be decided in a criminal trial. Legal guilt is different from moral guilt, delusional guilt, neurotic guilt etc.

620

Every act is a human act and no act is a crime unless it is viewed in that way by the law. Laws are changing and so do the crimes and concepts about crimes.

621

Never laugh at the crimes committed by others. What is there to laugh at the commission of crimes? Your own crimes may be a greater joke or tamasha for many.

622

A coffin-maker may be happy at the death of a human being. Never feel happy at the crimes committed by a fellow human being. Many people survive in the society because many people commit crimes.

623

Never use third degree methods to anyone in police custody. You will be sorry for everything you did when you see that he is dead in police custody.

624

Eighty six per cent of the problems during the investigation of crimes is caused by the tone of voice and other non-verbal cues during the transactions. The non-verbal signals during the interaction between the crime investigator and his witnesses / suspects / complainants / superiors / subordinates / prosecutors are very important for the success or failure of investigation work. Research studies show that 86 per cent of the communication during an interaction is through the non-verbal signals emanating from the people who are involved in transactions.

625

No police officer lasts more than his service-period, but his reputation or notoriety lasts for several years even after his retirement, death or termination from service.

626

No police officer can investigate a crime without sufficient knowledge about the law, crime and criminals. No police officer can redeem a criminal without knowing the mechanics of correction and rehabilitation.

627

No one ever becomes a criminal at once. There is a history of origin and development of criminal tendencies in him. Study the criminal from the background of his criminality and its growth.

628

No one really understands the grief or joy of a crime-doer. No criminal is as happy or as sorry as others think about him.

629

Behind every crime, there is a talent cancealed or expressed. Understanding the talent is the real efficiency of a police investigator.

630

No revolution can change the nature of man. Likewise, no police action can change the nature of man to commit crimes-on a permanent basis.

631

No news about a crimes lasts more than a few days. The crime is forgotten by the people, for, there comes the news of another crime in the meantime. What is there to wonder in the commission of an older crime when there comes the news of still more wonderful crimes in society?

632

The pressmen bring out the news and views about crimes. They do not have any sustained interest in any type of crimes. They are interested only in the news value of crimes and criminals. They are not bothered about the correction and rehabilitation of crime and criminals unless there is some news value in such matters.

633

No police officer thinks about a police investigator until he is accused in a crime. He speaks loudly how an investigation should be conducted justly, fairly and honestly when he is accused of a crime.

634

No act is criminal or non-criminal, but thinking makes it so.

635

Interpretation of an act as criminal is more important than the act itself. Any human act can be interpreted with some justification as criminal or non-criminal. On the same facts in issue, an accused is punished and on the facts in issue the same person is acquitted. It is the interpretation that matters.

636

Often, the greatest criminals lie unseen.

637

Police interrogators of little or no learning are always talkative during interrogation.

638

Pity a police station where every one is an interrogator.

639

Respect the law-keeper, but respect the law-breaker even

CHILDREN THROW STONES AT TREES ON THE WAYSIDE OR BELONGING TO OTHERS. IT GIVES PLEASURE TO THEM AND THEY KNOW THAT THEY ARE DOING WRONG THINGS. YET THEY DO IT. WHY?

more. For, the latter needs more understanding and help from you.

640

Judge a crime-doer by his attitude to crimes and not by his acts of criminality.

641

Keep the mouth shut and eyes wide open while interrogating a suspect. Non-verbal communication signals are more important than verbal signals.

642

A crime investigator reveals his character very vividly when he prepares his final report after investigation of a crime. He wants to administer justice, but he does not think how he can do so if he prepares his final report in the way he does !

643

Crimes are of different types—biological, psychological, financial, political, communal, or any such—The causes for each type may be many and different from one another. No theory of crime causation can answer all types of crimes and no theory of police approach can bring out the truth behind all sorts of crimes. Adopt different approaches to different types of crimes and criminals.

644

No man knows clearly what motivates him to commit a crime in a particular way. There are conscious and unconscious forces operating in every crime-doer. Likewise, there are many environmental factors operating upon him. Then, why search for the motive behind the commission of crimes?

645

Known to self and known to others—known to self but unknown to others—unknown to self but known to others—unknown to self and unknown to others—These are the four areas of human behaviour. Nobody can therefore say with certainty why one behaves the way he does. Some people commit crimes without knowing why they do so.

646

Multiple personality expresses in criminal behaviour. Some decent people sometimes utter indecent words. Why? A man has many personalities in him. Some of them are criminal and some others are not. Police officers too are no exception to this general rule.

647

To commit a crime without being detected is not an easy task. Ninetynine per cent of success in the successful commission of a crime is persperation. And ninetynine per cent of success in the successful detection of the crime is also persperation.

648

Earlier, the objective of imprisonment was purely punitive; later it became peno-correctional and now it has been well accepted that the aim of incapaciation of a citizen is for his correction and rehabilitation. Yet, we retain the nomenclature of the old school of thought and as a result, those citizens who are committed to correctional institutions are called prisoners and are thus looked down upon as convicts or better the convicted criminal. What an unfortunate state of attairs indeed!

649

Prisons, prisoners, jails, warders, jailors—all these nomenclatures have a punitive taste. Why not they be changed to inmates, correctional institutions, correctional centres, custodial assistants, correction-officers etc. Introduction of these new terms and designations will surely help the inmates and the staff to feel that their duties are not confined to punishment or custodial functions alone, rather, the imprisonment and custodial functions are means to a nobler aim which is nothing but correction.

650

The inmates in any correctional institution must start to feel that they are getting treated. This feeling is essential and important for correcting the inmates who are to readjust with the society and its norms when they are released.

651

Historically, the correctional institutions in India have, indeed, travelled a long way—yet, they are more custodial in nature. Between the custodial and correctional aspects of the inmates under the State care, the custodial aspects done alone have become the matters of serious concern for the administration. The staffing pattern clearly reflects a bias in favour of the custodial functions. In many countries, nearly 30 per cent of the staff in correctional institutions are correctional staff whereas in many institutions in India, the correctional staff are around 5 per cent or even less. This is a deplorable state of affairs and should be changed.

652

In view of the emphasis given to treatment, reformation and rehabitation, should we not restructure the staffing pattern of the correctional institutions in such a way that the ratio between the custodial and correctional personnel is meaningful enough to effect an attitudinal transformation in the inmates towards law and law-abiding nature of human beings? Should coercion and abridgement of human rights inherent in the punitive philosophy of the jail system be permitted to dominate the prison atmosphere by retaining the custodial staff in an abnormally large manner ?

653

Many detinues in police lock-ups or in judicial custody do not know the rules and regulations. Likewise, the rules and regulations relating to prison discipline are not taught to or told to the new entrants to correctional centres. Why are the new comers kept in blissful ignorance of these rules? The reasons are said to be—

1. The ignorance of the rules is the best way to subdue the new comers to the wishes of the custodial staff.
2. The new prisoner can be accused of for anything he does and can be victimized/given punishments for violating the prison rules or in the pretext of having violated the rules.

MASOCHISM
EVEN LITTLE CHILDREN COMMIT
SUICIDE : WHY ?
AGGRESSIVENESS DIRECTED TO
SELF!

3. Besides the prison staff, the older inmates too can subdue the new commers or victimize them.

What a tragedy indeed?

654

It is a fact to be accepted in all fairness that a good many members of the prison staff are only moderately educated or are lacking professional knowledge and training. Some of them are ill-informed about the philosophy, principles and modality of correctional administration, yet they behave as if they are the "kown-all" in correctional administration!

655

Even today, the Duckling Theory that a police or jail functionary learns to swim while he is on the job seems to dominate the thinking of the higher ups in prison (not correctional) administration and/or police. Resultantly, the police do not and can not function properly and scientifically. The professional background of the prison functionaries does not seem to instill in them the required confidence to correct the erred/erring inmates.

656

Many do not know why? Because of several reasons and owing to a cynical attitude, many prison officials are not inclined to equip themselves with adequate professional knowledge by way of training and education. "A criminal afterall" attitude is taken and the prison staff treats them as condemned people?

657

Both police and correctional staff should know the reformatory ideals and correctional policies. Both are related and together they form a triangular contact with the crime-doers. They should develop in them the correct aptitude, orientation, professionalism and above all the gift of human understanding and empathy.

658

Tension in many correctional institutions originate, many a time, out of the disputes over food and more so on the quality of food served. Suicidal deaths in police lock-ups are sometimes linked to the non supply of food to the detinues.

659

How well the food is prepared? The detinues in police stations do not ask this question. But, the inmates in jails do ask that question. How much food is given? Almost all detainees and more than 35 per cent of the inmates in correctional institutions find the quantity of food insufficient. Many of the crime-doers who are handled by police or by the correctional administration are more concerned with the quality of food than the nutritious value of the food contents. This is more so among the people in police lock-ups.

660

Research studies show that the inmates in correctional institutions do not get food for a second time or if at all they get, they have to do a lot of things which people outside do not know. The price to be paid for getting more or additional food may range from becoming a passing homosexual to the humouring of the staff/inmates who distribute food in the jail. What a deplorable state of affairs indeed!

661

Government provides food for the inmates in prisons and police lock-ups. There is a diet-scale prescribed for the inmates in prisons. No such diet or diet-scale may be seen in police stations. Why? The police too detain people in their custody for several days and don't they need a diet-scale?

662

As there is no diet-scale in police stations, the detainees in police lock-ups get food as the police like them to have it. The diet-scale in correctional institutions is found to be inadequate/ insufficient for many inmates. Does it mean that there exists some pilferage/underhand dealings in the supply of food materials. Some inmates do have suspicion about the underhand dealings.

663

Research studies show that almost all inmates in correctional institutions have money with them in varying amounts. The long termers keep larger sum of money with them. The inmates need money for a number of things which may include—chewing tobacco, smoking cigarettes, purchase of soaps, hair-oil or even addictive drugs. The administration seems to be blissfully ignorant of these? Why?

664

Researches show that the inmates need money to pay to their fellow inmates in the kitchen to get better or more food. Still others may require money to bring a passive homosexual for sexual abuse. The administration seems to be ignorant of these things? Why?

665

How does the money reach the inmates? There are two ways. (1) relatives and friends pass on cash during their interviews. (ii) the staff in the institution function as agents between the inmates and their relatives/next of kin/family members for collecting money. What a deplorable condition indeed!

666

Token wages are given to the inmates and presently it is, in some jails, in the range of Rs. 1/- to Rs 4/- for a day's hard work. There is an international understanding or consensus reached through the United Nations regarding the wages to be paid to the inmates who labour in correctional institutions. Should we still exploit the weakness of the inmates and extract hard work from him without paying anything ?

667

"The prisoner must receive proper remuneration and so far as possible, should be entitled to the benefit of the rights and prerogatives to which persons employed in freedom in similar employment are entitled outside the institution". According to the guidelines given by the United Nations, the wage structure in many countries has been changed. Should we not do it?

668

Don't the fallen brethren in custody deserve realistic wages for the hard labour they do?—particularly in view of the several philosophical and pragmatic considerations as well as court ruling in this regard? Does the payment of realistic wages after extracting real labour under custodial and controlled conditions become a charity or a right of the inmates?

669

'To deny a prisoner reasonable wages in return for his work will be to violate the mandate of Article 23(1) of the Constitution'—observe the courts in India. "If a fair wage is given, the State can absolve itself of the charge that it is exploiting the prisoners by taking free labour which, for a civilized government is certainly not commendable"—the courts observe further and say more emphatically that "a prisoner does not forfeit his citizenship nor does he lose civil rights except such rights as freedom of movement."

670

Should the family and the dependents of the inmate suffer for the crime one has committed? It may be a hard proposition to say 'let everyone suffer' and therefore a better approach will be to give a part of the wages he earns to the family/dependents.

671

Is the work-in a correctional institution-meant to carry out the FIATS of rigorous imprisonment and extract hard labour without paying reasonable wages to the inmates? Reasonable wages are always higher than the minimum wages and what is there to talk about it when the governments are not prepared to make changes in the wage structure?

672

What is the earthly utility of doing some useless jobs in prisons? It appears that many vocational training and trades currently offered in jails have outlived their relevance and therefore should be dropped. Many more trades should be added and most certainly in line with the occupational pattern and labour market demands outside the prison community.

673

Prison labour is still meant more for the benefit of the prisons—prison security and carrying out the fiats of rigorous imprisonment and not at all for the reformation or rehabilitation of the inmates. The police, the prison staff and the people do not seem to know the purpose of prison labour. What a pity indeed!

674

Generally, a prisoner is quite reluctant to take up the job/ trade for which he is trained in the institution once when he is released. This is owing to several caste/sub-caste/community, social and psychological reasons. If this is a truth, then why do we do these ritualistic exercises and waste our money, material and personnel. Teach the inmates some useful trade or industry.

675

Since the work assigned to the prisoner has no potential for getting an employment outside the prison or making a livelihood, most of the prisoners think that the trade taught or the work given to them in jails is to punish them and not for any useful or correctional purpose.

676

Institutionalization has four objectives—1. restraint of the convicted offenders, 2. their reformation and correction, 3. their rehabilitation after release and 4. their reintegration into the society.

677

Should we still stick to the 19th century organizational views relating to prison life? Custody, security, prison—discipline, institutional law and order, prison-labour, prison-education, work-programme etc. are still dominated by the notions of 19th century incarceration. Should we not change these time-worn objectives?

678

Researches show that the best incentive for an inmate in a correctional institution is to put the advancement of the day of

— CRIMINAL NEXUS—Vohra
BUREAUCRAT
POLITICIAN
BUSINESS MAN

his release to his own hands and giving remission is found to be one of the best in that direction.

679

"Ticket to leave system"—i.e., temporary leave from the correctional institution by which the inmates in a correctional institution showing good conduct are sent home for short period— should be widely employed.

680

In the treatment approach and in the correctional philosophy behind incarceration, ticket to leave system helps the prisoner to strengthen his ties with his family and friends. The system is found to be so essential for effective rehabilitation. It helps to curb down sexual perversions in the jails. Some prisoners may abscond and others may not be 'safe' to be sent under the ticket to leave system. As a result, the rules governing of the grant of the ticket to leave are so strict that even eligible prisoners find it extremely difficult to go home for short periods. Data in hand shows that the number of inmates who abscond while they are on ticket to leave are so small that there is the necessity of liberalising the rules and procedure for granting ticket to leave to the inmates in correctional institutions. Ultimately, an inmate has to rejoin his family/society and for it, the system pays rich dividends.

681

Parole means the release of an inmate from a correctional institution after he has served a part of his sentence. In many states in India, parole has not received due consideration. Why are we still reluctant to pass a special legislation on parole? Studies show that a good many parolees become successful in life and they do not become recidivists. Why don't we become more liberal in granting parole?

682

Prisoners should be released at the best time from the jails as such a release can help the inmates of correctional institutions to adjust better in society. Liberalize parole procedures.

683

Half—Way Homes are intermediate residential stations between prison life and freedom under supervision in society. In the west, many residential treatment centres or half-way houses have been developed and such houses provide food, shelter, counselling, guidance, care, supervision etc. for released inmates from correctional centres. The released prisoners work during the day and return to half-way houses after their working hours. When the released inmates acquire adequate inner controls and establish good contact in the community, they leave the half-way houses and live in society with more adjustment and happiness.

684

The offences enumerated in the Prison Rules seem to be such that any human act can be subjectively interpreted as a violation of the rules. Redrafting the entire chapter on offences and punishments in the Prison Rules with an aim to correct the inmates becomes necessary now.

685

Research studies show that there exits a state of confrontation between prisoners and officers in custodial institutions. The prison staff uses coersive and abusive tactics or speak insulting language/filthy expressions at the inmates so much so that any ordinary man is likely to get irritated or annoyed at them. How to stop this malady?

686

The inmates of a correctional institution do not like the police officers who see to it that they are put behind the bars. Hence, many of them do not have any favourable disposition to the police uniform which is deterrent and retributive to the inmates. As such, a change in the uniform of the prison staff resembling more on the correctional philosophy rather than policing the institution may be a welcome innovation.

687

The Staff-Inmate relationship is far away from being

satisfactory. The prison staff consider the inmates as 'prisoners afterall'. As such, they look down upon them and conspicuously keep a distance from them in the name of prison security. The inmates, in turn, try to become closer with the prison staff and as a result some of the inmates try to corrupt the prison-staff in various ways. There exists a state of confrontation between the staff and the inmates in case the latter fail to or refuse to humour the prison staff through corrupt practices.

688

One of the popular past time of the inmates is chatting together. Among other things, this becomes an effective and efficient channel of communication. Though in theory, there are a number of leisure-time activities in correctional institutions—e.g., reading, playing games, taking part in physical exercises, participating in cultural activities etc.—the fact remains that leisure time activities are not encouraged in the way they should be. The tragic result is that gossip becomes a necessary way of recreation for the inmates. Their favourite topics during their leisure-time are their superior officers, their doings, misdoings, favouritism, partiality, food, quality of food, corruption, crimes, methods of committing crimes etc. What to do and how to go about making the inmates to effectively utilize their time has never become a topic of serious concern for authorities.

689

The jail has a Board of visitors comprising both official and non-official members. The Jail Rules lay down clearly the authority and functions of jail visitors. One wonders whether or not the visitors are aware of their authority and functions. The interest of the visitors to our jails had been hitherto indifferent and this fact can be understood if one looks into the number of visitors to the jails--both central and sub-jails.

690

Research studies show that a few people convicted and jailed are innocent ones. Doubtlessly, they are the victims of miscarriage of justice.

691

The fundamental question is whether or not an inmate in a

INVESTMENT
FRAUDS...........
BAIT AND TRAP
INVESTMENT SCHEMES OFFERING FIFTY PER CENT INTEREST...........
DOUBLING OF THE PRINCIPAL AMOUNT WITHIN TWO YEARS.............
ENSURING OF GIFTS AND INCENTIVES TO THE INVESTORS........
AND THE INTENTION IS TO COMMIT FRAUDS ON PEOPLE......

correctional institution continues to be a citizen. Yes, he is. He has all fundamental rights, civil rights and human rights unless they are restrained by civilized law.

692

Should the undertrials who are detained under judicial custody be kept in jails manned by the prison department? No, They should not be housed under executive custody. Judicial custody means judicial custody and therefore the detention centres of the undertrials should be manned by judicial officers.

693

Custodial deaths are found to be more in correctional institutions than what they are in police lock-ups. Why? The reasons should be identified.

694

The undertrials account for nearly 70 per cent of the prison population today. Does it mean that the prisons are meant more for detaining the undertrials than correcting the convicted?

695

Undertrials spend their time in prisons without doing anything. No programme for correcting them can be initiated as they are not convicted ones. There are many undertrials who spend months and years in jails wasting money from public exchequer. Why should they be detained the way they are kept today?

696

Lock-ups—whether they are of police or of the prison department—should be clean and hygenically suitable for human dwelling.

697

'Bail hostels' on the lines of those sponsored and financed by Xenia Field Foundation, England, should be constructed in India.

698

The rights of the undertrial prisoners should be protected.

They have a right to wear their clothings, to eat their food and to have access to legal counsel, aid and things of like nature.

699

Any undertrial prisoner who spends long span in a jail should be released immediately and unconditionally.

700

There should be more open prisons constructed in any State.

701

There should be a 24 hours hot line service in all prisons to get in touch with authorities on human rights violations in prisons.

702

Police officers who were convicted for causing custodial deaths have become the head of the department—of police or of the correctional services. The complaint against them is that they too do not understand the crime-doers in the way in which they should.

703

Prisons were constructed in India with an intention of retribution and punishment—the purpose now being to correct the individual convicts with despotic discipline! The state of affairs continue even now and will continue for several years to come.

704

Macaulay (1838) recommended increased rigorous labour for the prisoners. He thought that imprisonment could make a terror in the mind of wrong doers. Decades have gone by and imprisonment could not make much terror in the minds of the wrong doers. Crimes continued to grow up and still continuing.

705

After Macaulay (1838), a second Committee was appointed in 1884. This Committee was instrumental for the enactment of the Prisons Act in 1894. Anglo-saxon administration of jails thus creeped into India through the Prisons Act and yet crimes continued to grow up and still continuing to grow.

706

In 1930, the third Committee, the Indian Jail Committee was appointed. Accordingly came the idea—the prisoners must be taught the latest methods and techniques to make them fit for finding out an honest and decent living after their release. What happened afterwards? Carpentary, smithy, weaving, soap-making, tailoring etc. are being taught even now to help the prisoners to find out a job for them!

707

In 1980, Mulla Committee was appointed. Mulla Committee recommended radical reforms of Indian prisons and a better life for the inmates in correctional institutions. In 1986, the National Expert Committee on Women Prisoners was appointed and the Committee recommended for a radical and humanist technology of custodial justice. What is the impact of the recommendations is yet to be seen.

708

Some estimates show that there are about 2 lakhs of prisoners in India housing in about 1156 prisons and 85 central jails. This may further mean that the prisoners' problems are national issues affecting several lakhs of people who are the dependents/next of kin of the convicted in jails.

709

'You can not polish a tile into a precious stone'—This is a Japanese proverb. Some jail authorities say that one can not correct recidivists. Of course, one can not polish a tile into a precious stone, yet one can polish it to have better appearance. Likewise, even a recidivist can be polished. Why don't you try for it?

710

You can not correct a convict by talking about it. You have to do something for it and do it now.

Consumerism and Dowry Deaths

IT IS NOT THE NEED BUT THE GREED WHICH MAKES PEOPLE TO COMMIT DOWRY DEATHS.

BOTH MEN AND WOMEN ARE RESPONSIBLE FOR IT.

711

"You cannot see Heaven without dying yourself"—This is a Hindi proverb. Likewise, one can not see the inner workings of a crime-doer's mind unless you make attempts to understand him.

712

You don't expect a prisoner to nod his head when you speak to him—that will be done only by your shadow and not the prisoner. The prisoner is a human being with flesh and blood.

713

"You may thank god that people commit crimes and are sent to you for correction. What is your qualifications to correct a crime-doer? What is your merit to do so? What is your eligibility to be so? "You are a blessed man and I am a condemned prisoner"—thought a prisoner in this way.

714

Your cruelty should not exceed the prisoner's capacity to tolerate you.

Punishment should not exceed the prisoner's capacity to bear.

CHAPTER - 7

CRIME AND HUMANITY : IS THE CRIME-DOER HUMAN ?

715

There must be some reason for a person to commit a particular crime. Yesterday, he did not—and—tomorrow he may not commit a crime. Yet today, he committed and thus he was detected. The fact that he was not detected so far showed that he was not altogether devoid of human qualities and sense of justice.

716

Some studies show that criminals and delinquents behave as they do because they are either "sick" or "maladjusted". The same studies are equally applicable to police as well. They too behave as they do because they too are either "sick" or "maladjusted" if their behaviour is violative of their code of conducts.

717

Criminality may be the expression of a person's psyche. The environments in which he is placed may work as a precipitating cause for the expression of criminality. The police, to understand the crime better, must study the predisposing and precipitating factors in psyche of a crime-doer. But, how many police officers are competent to do so ?

718

If a suspect under police custody is found to suffer from mental pathology, he deserves consideration and sympathy. If he is treated cruelly, it means that the people who treat him in that way suffer from more severe mental pathology.

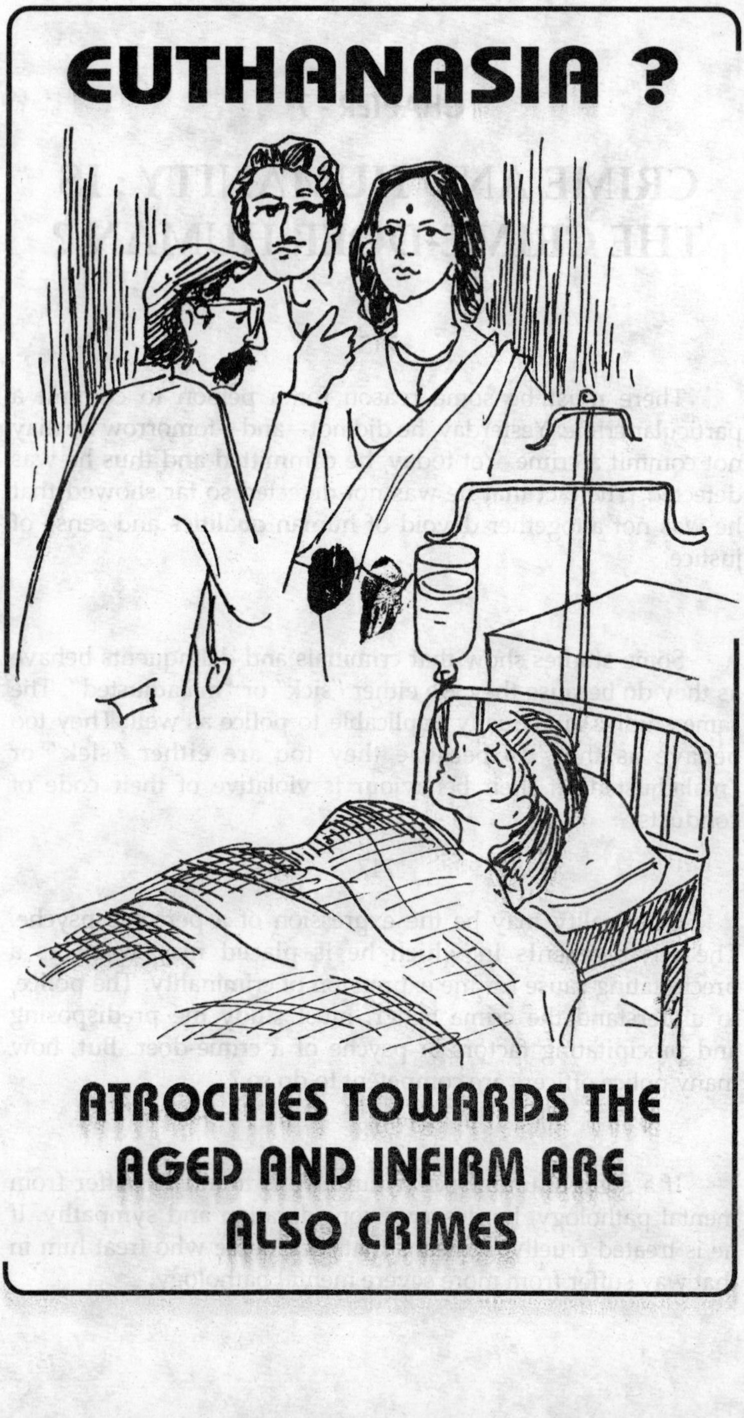
EUTHANASIA ?
ATROCITIES TOWARDS THE AGED AND INFIRM ARE ALSO CRIMES

719

Studies conducted show that 80-85 per cent of the criminals handled by the police, prosecutor and the courts are normal people. Some may be found to suffer from mild forms of personality maladjustments.

720

Psychoanalytic school thinks that human behaviour which includes criminal behaviour is largely the product of unconscious psychological-biological forces called 'drives or instincts'. Criminal behaviour arises out of conflicts related to these basic drives.

721

The extent of criminals suffering from psychotic disorders is no greater than the same among the 'so named' non criminals. Some studies show that psychoses are less common among offenders. The detected criminals represent a cross-section of the society as far as their mental disorders are concerned.

722

Police represent a cross section of the society. What is good in society in seen is police as well as in the general public. What is bad is also seen similarly. Studies conducted show that there is no difference between the members in police service as well as the members in the general public as far as criminal tendencies among the two groups are concerned.

723

"Behaviour of criminals" or "criminality of behaviour"– which is more important for police. Criminality of behaviour is important to identify criminal behaviour and the behaviour of criminals is important to decide the manner of treatment to him. For the police, both are important.

724

It is very difficult to say precisely when Indian criminology began. Nevertheless, there are references about the causative, preventive, punitive, deterrent, reformative, correctional, investigative aspects of crime in ancient books—Ramayana,

Mahabharata, Arthasastra etc. But, they were not dealing with crimes in a scientific way. Even now one doubts whether or not the people and the police in India give due importance and prominance to the study of criminology although everyone of them deals with crime and criminals in different capacities.

725

People violate norms. No norm is universal or unchanging and therefore today's crime may be tomorrow's virtue.

726

A human act becomes a criminal act because many people want it to be called criminal. What was called virtue yesterday may become a crime tomorrow.

727

Anybody can become a crime-doer, for, criminality is not the family property of anybody.

728

Anybody can make anybody to become a criminal. Provide situations in such a way that the other can not but behave like a criminal or become a criminal.

729

Master of a situation—servant of a situation—victim of a situation. In all the three situations, one can become a crime-doer.

730

There are crimes known to others and to self ; known to self and unknown to others ; unknown to self and known to others; and unknown to self and to others. What to do ?

731

How many people know the penal laws of the Country and the ingredients of the sections of law to make his act as a crime defined in the penal law ? Yet, the principle is 'ignorance of law is not an excuse'— Rediculous indeed !

732

'Ignorance of law is no excuse'— this principle is accepted in jurisprudence not to save the innocent man who is ignorant of the laws, but to catch hold of any person who commits an offence. The law does not want him to take the plea that he did not know the law. At the same time, the principle in jurisprudence is : "Let a thousand criminals go unpunished, no innocent person should be punished". How can these two principles go together ?

733

Victim-participation and victim-precipitation may be two factors responsible for the commission of crimes. The penal law which was written in 1860 did not take note of these latest concepts in victimology. Why to think in this way ? Many of the concepts during 1860 about crimes are no longer applicable today in the changed melieu. Yet, the time-worn and antique laws are applied to administer justice !

734

The Indian Penal Code is a museum piece and yet the provisions are used to catch criminals. Research studies show that nearly 17 sections in the Penal Code are of some use today. The rest are only sparingly used and altogether only 100 penal sections of the Indian Penal Code are of some relevance now. The rest are useless, inoperative and rusted.

735

People are not worried about crimes so long as they themselves are not hurt, affected or inconvenienced by them.

736

No behaviour is universally and eternally condemned by the people in all cultures all over the world. The same principle is applicable to criminal behaviours as well.

737

No criminal lives by bread alone. He too desires recognition, acceptance, love, care, security and he finds them in the world of crime.

738

People interact and the fundamental ways in which people interact are called social processes. Cooperation and opposition

FREEDOM MAKES PEOPLE HAPPIER....
NO CONVICT IS HAPPY IN A JAIL
NO FISH IS HAPPY IN AN ACQUARIUM
NO BIRD IS HAPPY IN A CAGE
NO HOUSE-WIFE IS HAPPY AT HOME WHEN HER HUSBAND IS IN A JAIL
PUNISHMENT IS MORE FOR THE DEPENDENTS THAN TO THE CONVICTS

are the two basic social processes. Differentiation, stratification, accommodation and assimilation are the social processes (They arise from cooperations and oppositions) and they operate in all forms of human behaviour—criminal as well as non-criminal.

739

All kinds of people from all walks of life commit crimes. Many people are able to escape from being caught and they accuse those unfortunate people who have become victims of legal action as criminals.

740

White-collar crimes, Blue-collar crimes, No-collar crimes, khaki-collar crimes ...... conventional criminality, convictional criminality, enforcement criminality .... cognizable crimes, non-cognizable crimes, political crimes, economic crimes, organised crimes, socio-economic crimes .... and thus the crimes are of many kinds and varieties. Criminal behaviour, like all human behaviour, must be studied through the co-operation of many disciplines each making use of its concepts and specialized techniques.

741

Family is the primary group in which the human relations are intimate and face to face. Infact, it is the primary agency of social control and in that way it controls human behaviour including criminal behaviour. In India, decline of the primary groups is weakening as an important agency of social control. The laws and law courts are taking up the role of families. The result is increase of disruption in family life and consequent divorces in marital life.

742

Every society changes and the changes tend to upset the balance of social relationships and to introduce new and conflicting values. The result will be social disorganisation whose onset will be marked by the increase of social problems including crime and delinquency.

743

There may be socially induced deviations—i.e., deviations which the culture and social organization together produce.

Dowry deaths, caste-discriminations, untouchability, child marriage etc. may be examples in point. The police do not have much to do with these social maladies.

744

'Normality' is a concept and 'abnormality' is a reality. Logically therefore, normal behaviour is only a concept and abnormal behaviour is a reality. It follows therefore that crime is a reality in all societies.

745

Multitude of factors of different kinds may be responsible for causing crime and delinquency. Many of such factors are beyond the control of individuals living in the society. It may be accepted that many of the factors responsible for causing crimes in society are beyond the control of police. Legal measures taken by police to prevent crimes may not have any impact upon the prevention of crime.

746

If the police are not vigilant and active, the crimes may increase. This is a wrong proposition. In the absence of police, the society will create its own strategies to control and prevent crimes. Organised policing is of recent origin. Even before, the society took care of itself.

747

'Policy often effects where force cannot'— This is a wise saying. The role of police in enforcing the provisions of many social legislations is indeed nominal. Violations of the provisions of social legislations should be handled by a policy change and creation of an awareness for change. Police force, however strong it may be, can not be a substitute for policy change.

748

A person who lives by committing crimes can not have a natural death. His dead body may be seen in a gutter or on the road-side or in a river or as an anonymous corpse etc.

749

Crime is a constant in any society. There should be a quantum of crime for all societies. All societies therefore produce certain number of crimes.

750

Every society has values and criminal values and therefore there will be a group of people who cling to the criminal values thinking that they are the only values which may ensure social welfare. They surely violate the values and embrace criminal values.

751

There is a school of thought which speaks of violence prone personality. So long as such people live, there will be violent personal crimes.

752

A sub-culture of violence can be seen in some societies—particularly in urban settings wherein goondaism, hired murderers, underworld criminals and so on live and flourish. Criminologists may say that it is a sign of developing society in any culture.

753

Commission of many crimes is remunerative and therefore it is difficult to control many of the crimes simply by moral exhortations, ethical inhibitions, or by the force of public opinions.

754

Commission of certain types of crimes is regarded in many quarters as respectable—ensuring status and financial stability. People have acquisitive urge.

755

Government officials misuse government vehicles for private use, make use of government telephone for personal purpose, take government's stationary for home use, utilize the subordinates to do works for them etc. The misuse of authority and misappropriation of government property etc. are not

Delinquent Boys
Kamath
SOME CHILDREN FIND PLEASURE IN EMPTYING THE AIR IN CYCLES BELONGING TO OTHERS AND THEREBY TO CAUSE TROUBLES FOR OTHERS
SADISM ?

considered as crimes but only as misconducts. If they are not crimes, then what are they ?

756

People speak of under-world criminals and upper-world criminals. What is the difference between the two ?

757

Claiming of false travelling allowance, evading of tax, misappropriation of government property, misuse of government machinery, corrupt practices, fortune making by government job etc. are various ways by which criminal tendencies are expressed by government servants. Yet, they are treated like law abiding citizens !

758

When the crimes committed by government servants are taken into account, some studies show that some of them are "habitual criminals". But, they are not caught because they perform government jobs and they can afford to commit crimes without being caught or if at all caught, their crimes are called only 'misconducts' with no penal sanction of imprisonment or death penalty.

759

Corporate crimes are criminal acts of corporations and individuals acting in their corporate capacity. "It refers specifically to illegal acquisitive behaviour engaged in for the immediate purpose of increasing corporate (as distinguished from personal) wealth" (J.T. Carey).

760

What is called 'occupational crimes ?' Any crime committed by a person during the course of his occupational activities is called occupational crimes.

761

Electricity is produced by the State Electricity Boards—the road transport is conducted by the State Transport Corporations— the water is purified and distributed by the State Water

Authority—the telephones and communication are managed by special departments—letters are to be delivered by the postal authorities. All these Boards, Corporations, Authorities, departments do not perform their duties promptly and properly and the general public suffer. What type of crimes are they ? No Board, Corporation, Authority and Department consider that they indulge in committing crimes when their services are denied except for justifiable reasons.

762

One may observe occupational crimes from the peon to the chief secretary to the government, from the security guard to the managing director, from the constable to the director general of police. What to do and how to go about them for controlling the extent and intensity of occupational crimes without adversely affecting the bureaucratic and administrative set up—is a problem now.

763

The public pay little or no attention to the occupational crimes of the bureaucrats. This is so because the public reaction is likely to invite more troubles to them. Life will then become miserable as the people may be denied of the basic necessities in life if they start reacting to bureaucratic crimes.

764

Bureaucratic crimes are those crimes which the members of the bureaucracy commit during the course of their bureaucratic works. Hoarding of files, delaying of decisions, causing of more troubles, putting matters into a state of indecision, raising unnecessary querries etc. are considered as bureaucratic crimes.

765

"How a favourable decision should not be given"—this becomes a motivating factor for many of the bureaucratic crimes. For it, the rules, regulations and laws are, sometimes, misinterpreted and it gives a lot of pleasure for the bureaucratic criminals. Every department, corporation, board, company, authority, enterprise will have a group of bureaucratic criminals.

766

One of the most serious problems confronting Indian society is that of the bureaucratic criminals. Besides bribery, corruption, misuse of authority, exercise of pseudo-authority, hoarding of files, they establish underhand dealings with politicians and businessmen. Politicians, business-men and bureaucrats together can cause havoc in the world of criminality.

767

It may be argued that money and women are the basis of most crimes. Now, it is accepted that bureaucratic powers also is at the root of some crimes.

768

Thousands of people handled by the police, prosecutors, the courts and prison—authorities may be first offenders or better situational criminals. A situational criminal is one who commits a crime because of the pressures of circumstances.

769

A situational criminal does not mean that the crime has been committed all on a sudden—without any premeditation. Some people commit crimes—of course, owing to pressures circumstances—after brooding over the commission of crimes. Hence a situational criminal need not be one suffering from pathological disorders.

770

There are people who commit suicide after premeditating well about the means to be adopted. There may be a suicide-pact made by the members of the entire family to commit suicide. In all senses, they are situational criminals.

771

Situational criminals are different from convictional criminals. People who belong to the suicide squads, Naxalite movements, terrorist activities are convictional criminals and therefore they claim that they commit crimes for common welfare of the society. But, situational criminals commit crimes—of-course, out of convictions—but not for the larger interest of the society. A situational criminal has only personal interests.

INVITING TROUBLES ?

NEVER COUNT MONEY IN PUBLIC;
IT IS AN INVITATION TO THIEVES AND
PICK-POCKETS

VICTIMOLOGY

772

As a rule, a person commits murder only once in his whole life, if murder is the motive behind the act. As murderers are not generally repeaters, their finger-prints are not taken and kept by the police. Many murderers, usually, are situational criminals.

773

Chronic criminals are offenders who commit crimes repeatedly. Among them, there may be petty thieves, pocket-pickers, burglars as well as corporate criminals, bureaucratic criminals, white-collar criminals and upper-class criminals.

774

Chronic criminals are of two categories— (1) those who have a feeling that they are committing crimes and (2) those who do not have such feelings. Pick-pockets, burglars and so on may belong to the first category and the bureaucratic criminals, white collar criminals and so on may belong to the second category.

775

Bureaucratic criminals are professionals in committing crimes. They know how to do things in such a way that they are not caught. They commit crimes for making money or for enjoying power, prestige, authority, pleasure or selfish achievements etc.

776

A bureaucratic criminal once wrote in his diary: "each act I do in my official work is a business proposition and so do my superior officers. Considered from the business angles and measured only by rupees and gains, the opportunity to commit crimes in my official career is more than what a professional criminal can get. He has to do everything under fear whereas I do not have to."

777

"A bureaucratic criminal makes crores of rupees—or that is what is unearthed by raids in these days"—said a professional thief once. "Ofcourse, a bureaucratic criminal has prestige and status whereas a professional thief does not have"—he continued.

778

Proneness to commit crimes in seen in all people. But, a person is called a recidivist only if he is found indulging repeatedly in the commission of conventional crimes—defined so by the statutes. White collar criminals, enforcement criminals, bureaucratic criminals, occupational criminals are also recidivists but they are not called so. Why ?

779

Criminologists may say that there is no real solution to crimes. People will continue to commit crimes and the police will continue to catch some of them. The prosecutors will continue to prosecute a few of them and the courts will continue to convict some of those "few" tried before them. And the process will continue till the consumation of the world.

780

Public order crimes include homosexuality, prostitution, drug-addiction, alcoholism, gambling, traffic offences, vagrancy, disorderly conduct, exhibitionism etc. Are they police problems ? What can the jail authorities do with social pathology ? They are community problems.

781

Crime is eternal—as external as humanity. Like disease, handicappedness etc., crime too is ever present in any society. Every man becomes sick sometimes in his life and so does he in the commission of crimes. A man who does not commit crimes lives only in a non-existent utopia.

782

A man may be able to live without food for a few days. But, he can not live without committing crimes—in thoughts, words or actions—even for a few hours.

783

How many people in society know the ingredients of the legal definition of a crime ? hardly a few. Yet, crimes are reported to the police and the first information reports are prepared. Often, the first information reports are prepared in such a way that there is violation of every ingredient of the law by the crime-doer ? The question is: "is there any violation of law even in the preparation of the F.I.Rs ? If there is, then what is that crime called ?"

784

A police constable is not expected to study much about the law. He is taught only the elementary aspects of law, procedure and evidence. But, he does catch hold of crime-doers with his little or no knowledge in law. Even in such instances, F.I. Rs are drafted and often it is so done by people who know the law and in such a way that everything the so named crime-doer did was a violation of the criminal law of the country. If the law-enforcement officer is not justified in what he does in the name of law enforcement, then what is it to be done ?

785

"Trial and Error Arrest"—what is this ? This is called taking people into custody in an informal way for questioning and interrogation until-atlast the police are able to find out and arrest the real criminals. "Trial and Error Arrests" are violations of the statutory provisions, but seldom do people object to such illegal practices. Human rights activitsts are now against this sort of "Trial and Error Arrests".

786

What is the wrong in employing third degree methods on a rapist ? Some police officers ask this question. They also ask: "What will be your attitude when you see that you are burglarised or your son has been kidnapped ?" Yes, there is a point in what the police officers speak about the use of third degree methods. Ofcourse, the victims of burglary or the parents of the kidnapped may tolerate or even encourage almost any illegal tactics in order to have the detection of crimes. Nevertheless, no police officer can or should defend such a position with any moral justifications for the illegal acts.

787

Criminologists do not and can not blame people for committing crimes. They further say that all enforcement officers

VICTIMOLOGY

VICTIMS OF CRIME AS
A CAUSE OF CRIME

SHE INVITES THIEVES.
LOOK AT THE ORNAMENTS AND
THEY ATTRACT CRIME-PRONE
PEOPLE.

are also human beings and therefore they do not blame them for committing crimes. At the same time, they insist that all people should accept the fact that crime is a human act and very much an act which all people commit in one way or another.

788

The Penal Codes prescribe punishments to offences and the punishments are generally in the form of fine or imprisonment. They are fixed as early an 1860 when the Penal Code was written in India. It appears that the inflation has not affected much on the imposition of fine on the guilty although it has affected a lot in deciding the fees to be paid to the lawyers. The penal code is hopelessly outdated.

789

The Indian Penal Code reflected the thinking of nineteenth century when criminology and penology were not born, or, if at all were just born, not much developed. It has served the country for nearly one and half a century. It has now become a museum piece. Accept the reality as it is.

790

"Crime is assignable to no single universal source, nor yet to two or three : it springs from a wide variety and usually from a multiplicity, or alternative and converging influences" (Cyril Burt).

791

What are the principal factors which influence a person to commit crimes. At least, one may see four factors in any specific case. They are—(1) The pre-disposing factors, (2) The precipitating factors and (3) The contributory factors and (4) factors present but not apparently found operative. Police officers, prosecutors, judges and prison-officials can not see all these push and pull factors unless they are properly trained in behavioural sciences and are open to appreciate the behavioural dynamics.

792

Restitution to the victims of the miscarriage of justice should be made a right of the victims. There are countries in the world which admit this principle.

793

"The legal bases for compensation to the innocent convict are : *first,* the right of eminent domain, that is, that the owner of private property taken for public use shall be compensated, for in these cases private liberty, a right atleast as sacred as that of property, has been taken by the State; *second,* the theory supporting the Workman's Compensation Act, that in the operation of any great undertaking, such as the management of a large industry, or the administration of criminal law, there are bound to be a number of accidents and that the accidents much be compensated" (Jorone Frank).

794

All police officers agree that there is no easy way to understand crimes. Both police and prison authorities admit that there is no quick and sure cure, remedy or relief for crimes.

795

Crimes can not be cured by committing crimes and therefore be just and honest in dealing with crimes and criminals. Enforcement criminality is worse than conventional criminality as the former category is committed by a mammoth law—enforcement agency and the latter by an individual.

796

The State can do no wrong. Hence, what can be done if a person is erroneously convicted or an innocent is incarcerated ? The law does not speak anything much about it. If the justice system errs, the system should award compensation. Then only the system will be just and fair.

797

From the point of view of ensuring more personal liberty and freedom from torture, the people in general feel: "the less the police have contacts with them, the better it is". Many do not want to become closer to police.

798

The suspects/detained have a lot of rights when they are in police custody. Researches show that police officers do not tell any of the rights which the suspects/detinues have in police stations. In every sense, the practice of not telling the rights of the suspects/detinues is unethical.

799

Organised police system is of recent origin. The Metropolitan Police in London was created only in 1829. All other police organizations in the world are of later origin. Even before orgainsed police was created, people used to commit crimes and the society found ways and means to manage and control criminals and their criminal activities.

800

Police have to catch criminals and they are trained for it. Studies show that Indian police are able to get hold of a small number of criminals even when crimes are reported to them. Why ? The detection rate is very low and deplorable.

801

Indian society has abundance of criminals in all descriptions and detection of crimes/criminals is just a function of the police today. Many police officers are not good investigators of crimes as they do not want to take the pain connected with crime investigation. Many criminals are highly mobile and police have only limited powers during the investigation of crimes and there are many such factors which make the police inefficient.

802

There exists citizen-hostility towards police in India. People show an avoiding attitude to police and the police show an authoritarian and often suspicious attitude to the citizens. If at all crimes are not proved, the citizens are not inclined to take up the bot' eration connected with crime investigation, prosecution and trail etc.

803

Every crime becomes a pclice baby. The citizens may always say: "punish the guilty, punish the guilty", but it appears that nobody comes forward either to punish the guilty or to save the innocent.

DETERRENT—RETRIBUTIVE ?

OR

PENO-CORRECTIONAL ?

I NEVER KNEW

WHAT HUMAN MISERY

WAS UNTIL I WAS LOCKED UP—A director general of police told it when he was released from a jail

804

It certainly cannot be said that police officers are revered people in India. People respect them out of fear and the fear is vanished at the first moment their power and authority are taken away.

805

Torturing people in public by the police may be justified as it has been done in public's visibility. But, torturing people in police lock-ups, police vehicles, away from pubic's visibility can not be justified. The police are accountable for their actions.

806

"What the Police Commission said in 1903 would more or less apply fully even to the present situation. If anything, the position has worsened with more rampant corruption in police today with active connivance of numerous local dadas and unprincipled men in public life" (National Police Commission).

807

Many cases, especially rape, molestation, sexual abuses etc, are likely to be acquitted by the courts of law after the trial. The culprits in such instances make fun of the legal machinery and system. Some police officers and members of the public, therefore, justify retributive justice to such sex perverts. Ofcourse, there is a point in their arguments and one finds moral justifications in such vindictive strategies. Yet, one may say that the police are not legally expected to take law into their hands and punish the guilty.

808

Many research studies may show that the people do not admire the policeman; yet one may see that they are the first ones to face risks when the public are in trouble. The statistics on police-casuality may show that attacks on policemen are on the increase.

809

Mooching (receiving of free gifts as a favour), chiselling (demanding free admission to events and entertainments) shakedown (appropriation of expensive items for personal use) and cooping (sleeping on duty and avoiding routine patrol duties) are found to be damaging the image of police among the public.

810

Some police officers say that the police in many developed and the developing countries are worse than Indian police in violation of human rights and in the use of torture against people. Their argument may be true, but it can not justify an otherwise illegal act. It can perhaps mitigate the seriousness of the police misbehaviours, but can never approve of them. If people in developed or developing countries commit murder of other fellow beings, it is bad and it can not be brought as a justification of murdering people here.

811

The police in developed countries and other developing countries have a lot of enviable qualities. Why not they be accepted and implemented here ?

812

Police work has elements of danger and authority. The working personality of a policeman, therefore, has—may have—some characteristics like suspiciousness and conservatism. Ofcouse, these characteristics make the police unpopular.

813

'Cop-mentality'—that is what people do not like. Many a policeman thinks that everyone approaching the police for help is a criminal and if the allegation is true, it can not develop good police—citizen relations.

814

Police are charged with the use of excessive force, brutality, torture, assaults of innocent people, violations of human rights, illegal use of violence in areas of civil rights demonstrations, communal disturbances, political demonstrations, campus unrest, journalists' encounters etc. Although some of the charges are exaggerated or overexaggerated, it can not be denied that the police use force in their dealings with citizens in which violence clearly exceeds the demands of the situations. Many commissions of enquiry instituted by the governments show that the public charges are not altogether baseless.

CHAPTER - 8

CRIME AND COURT : IS JUSTICE ADMINISTRATION FAIR ?

815

'JUST ICE' is called 'Justice'. Justice may be as cold as ice.

816

Justice has no eyes, no ears and no heart. But it has and should have all of them.

817

Justice is what crime-doer says—Justice is what the police say—Justice is what the people say—Justice is what the lawyers say—Justice is what the judge says and there is justice in what everybody says.

818

Poetic justice, police justice, prosecutor's justice, court's justice, people's justice and do they all mean the something in the same way ?

819

Criminal justice, victim justice, equal justice, crimino-victim justice and what do all these mean ? Is there any justice at all ?

820

Justice, justice everywhere, but not a just man anywhere.

821

Every criminal is just in one way and unjust in some other way. Likewise, the police reaction to the criminal is just in one

HUNGER BREAKS THROUGH STONE WALLS

WHEN POOR PEOPLE COMMIT CRIMES, POVERTY IS SAID TO BE THE CAUSE OF SUCH CRIMES — WHY ?

BUT

WHEN AFFLUENT PEOPLE COMMIT PROPERTY OFFENCES, AFFLUENCE IS NOT SAID TO BE THE CAUSE OF CRIME — WHY ?

way and unjust in some other ways. So are the reactions of the press, people, prosecutors and so on.

822

Justice is a nebulous term. Justice by conviction and the 'convicted' justice is turned to justice by acquittal in an appeal, revision or review. Then, what is this justice ? There are people who are condemned to suffer all these and taste the consequence.

823

Justice administration is a process and it begins when a person commits a crime and ends nowhere. Both acquittal and conviction do not ensure justice.

824

An acquittal means that a person accused to have committed an offence is found to be not guilty by law after several years of his having committed the crime as alleged by the police and prosecutors.

825

A conviction means that a person accused to have committed an offence is found to be guilty by law after several years of his having committed the crime as alleged by the police and prosecutors.

826

Everyman in any society is a victim of crime in some way and in every sense. The man who commits a crime and the agencies who deal with him for administering justice—all are victims of crime. Who is a greater victim ?

827

Justice is not a simple or single word. It is a paragraph. Miscarriage of justice' is a longer paragraph.

828

Can an acquittal or conviction be a cure to the crime one has committed ? No, they can not. Then, what are they ? They are the verdicts of a court of law. Nothing more, nothing less.

They do not have much to do with administration of justice, for, justice is entirely a different matter.

829

God's justice and that is the real-justice. But, nobody knows what it is.

830

Arrest, bail, remand, trial, jail etc. are the general prescriptions to all sorts of criminals from petty thieves to day-light robbers. Fine or imprisonment or both—They are the prescriptions for all sorts of crimes and criminals when convictions are awarded.

831

Fine, imprisonment, death, forefeiture of property—what a wonderful medicine to cure of the maladies of crimes in society ! On one side, medicines are prescribed and administered and on the other side, crimes are increasingly committed. The punishment is not a remedy or relief to the disease; yet it is awarded.

832

Can punishment control human behaviour—especially criminal behaviour ? Evidence in hand shows that crimes co-exist with punishments of all kinds and every description.

833

Who is concerned with the convicted ?—especially with those convicted of fine ? The convicted pay the fine and merrily go out to the society. Ofcourse, the fine has increased the revenue to the State. Money comes and money goes and the crime-doer considers the fine only in that way—nothing more and nothing less.

834

Treatment to a disease consumes a lot of money and some people consider the fine imposed upon them for the crime committed just as a necessary expenditure to get out of the legal clutches.

835

Investigation, detection, prosecution, trial, conviction, appeal, acquittal, second appeal, punishment—and how much time, energy, money and man-power are taken for all these processes to commence and to complete ? And what are the ultimate advantages when everything gets over after one or two decades ? Justice delayed is justice denied.

836

Every step during the investigation, prosecution, trial, incarceration involves money and expenditure—say the accused in crimes. For what do they spend money ? The money is spent to ensure justice and for them, it is an expensive affair. Many acquitted people have become paupers by the time they are acquitted and so are the cases with the convicted when they are punished. Is it administration of justice ?

837

Women want that crimes against them must be investigated by women police, argued by women prosecutors, tried by women judges and so on. Is it what is called "gender justice ?"

838

In some countries, women judges who try offences against women award lesser punishments to the offenders when compared to the punishments verdicted by men judges to offenders who commit offences against women. Why is it so ?

839

There was a time people thought that cutting off the hands, plucking off the eyes, chopping off the legs etc. were justice to the crime-doers. Later people thought that such methods were injustice. But nothing was done to remedy the injustice done to earlier criminals when it was accepted that earlier methods were not justice.

840

What was justice yesterday might not be justice today. And what is justice today may not be justice tommorrow. There is nothing called permanent justice.

841

Justice in one part of the world may be injustice in another part. Capital punishment is still considered to be justice by people in India whereas it is considered to be injustice in many countries. In Gulf countries, corporal punishments are not abolished whereas in India, they are abolished. If this is so, what is exactly justice ?

842

There was a time pocket-pickers were punished with death penalty. Now, people say that all pocket pickers should survive and get corrected. What a change in attitude and approach to pocket pickers. Nobody speaks anything for the departed souls of the people who became victims of an unjust approach.

843

One man decides the nature of justice. A king once saw that immersing the hands of the crime-doers in boiling oil was not justifiable and therefore he abolished the system in South India. Thereafter people said that the immersion of the criminal's hand in boiling oil was an injustice.

844

Man is the greatest persecutor of man and often he does it in the name of justice or in the pretext of administering justice to man.

845

Is justice elastic ? One man is punished for an offence for six months' imprisonment whereas another is given one year's of incarceration. Yet, a third one is awarded two years' of jail-life and what is the criteria in awarding sentences for people who commit the same kind of offences ?

846

Judicial discretion in awarding of punishment to crime-doers has become a subject of research in these days. The research findings show that the personality of the judges, their subjective views, opinions, prejudices, preconceived notions etc. affect their decision-making powers. At the receiving end of their decisions, one may see the acquitted or convicted as the case may be.

847

"Justice" and "Just Justice"—both are two concepts. Justice should be done—not only that—it should appear to people that justice has been done. Some crime-doers complain that they are sinned against more than sinning and if they are true when they say so, then it means that they do not get "JUST JUSTICE".

848

Fair justice and fairness in justice—both are two concepts. The former speaks about the nature of justice and the latter about the procedure in awarding justice. For ensuring "JUST JUSTICE", it is necessary to show fair justice and fairness in justice.

849

Nearly two lakhs of people are always in Indian jails. Nearly 3/4 th of them are undertrial prisoners. They suffer the penal stay, penal treatment, penal food etc. for obtaining justice in the case tried against them. And at the end of the trial, when they are acquitted, they have to forget about the sufferings they underwent in the prisons. Can they forget things as easily as people want them to forget ?

850

Today's society wants the correction of crime-doers. It thinks that corrective gustice is the JUST JUSTICE. For this, the crime-doers are sent to correctional centres. Society feels disheartened when it sees that recidivists are on the increase. Where is the defect ?

851

The judge thinks that he administers justice when he pronounces his judgement in each criminal case. The judgements of the judge is further judged by the police, prosecutors, people, press and the crime-doers. Each one of them makes his own judgements although none of them speaks out the judgements made over the judgements of the courts of law.

REFORMATION......

CORRECTION.......

REHABILITATION....

"PRISON IS AN INSTITUTION FOR CORRECTING CRIME-DOERS" — must surely has been written by a philanthropist and not at all by a jail administrator or by an inmate in the so named correctional institutions

THE CONVICTS HAVE DIFFERENCES OF OPINION

852

Deterrent justice, retributive justice, incapacitative justice, corrective justice and many people speak many things about justice. Nobody seems to mean much when they speak all these things as many are still ignorant of what exactly is the purpose of justice administration.

853

If the justice administration is still confused about the purpose of punishment, then why does it punish people ? Let it clarify the purpose/s first and let it implement its decision. Any decision executed under confusion will have only confused results and that is what is seen in hardened criminals, in repeaters of crimes and in recidivists.

854

One year's imprisonment and several year's harassment. Is it administration of justice ?—asked a crime-doer. In some States in India, the conviction rate is only 8 per cent of the total crimes reported. This is the position in the trial court and the conviction rate lowers down in the first court of appeal to 2 per cent. If this is true, the harassment is the punishment to crime-doers.

855

Recollection of past sorrow may be joyful for many—but not for the crime-doers. An acquittal can not and does not make man joyful and he will have the hang over of the untold miseries, social humiliations, financial crises etc. for several years even after the pronouncement of the acquittal verdict.

856

Glamour of the power of a judge remains with him only till he pronounces the judgement. Be judicious.

857

The police, prosecutor, judge and the people entrust a convicted person to authorities in correctional institutions and thereafter what happens to him ? Some people treat him as the last, least and the lost. Is he so ?

SMALL FAMILY
The same criminal tendencies are seen in man, woman and children. There is no difference in kind, although there may be differences in degrees.

858

Crime-doer is an individual and the police is a legion. The laws are written in such a way that the 'legion' can enforce them on the individual. Individual's interest should be protected and if it is not protected, what can an individual do ? — suffer ? A crime-doer often prefers not to react as reaction is likely to bring more hardships and agonies on him.

859

No man commits a crime desiring someone to catch him. No man goes to jail desiring for correction.

860

Steal a purse and you are a thief; steal a country and you are a king. People will start adoring you.

861

If there were no criminals on earth, the enforcement officers will make some, for, their survival depends upon the number of criminals they handle.

862

If crime-doers did not exist, all the police, prosecu ors, defence lawyers, courts, jails in the world have no meaning and relevance.

863

"If you wish to avoid seeing a criminal, you must first break your mirror" — says.Guruji to police, prosecutors and jail authorities.

864

If you want to correct a man convicted to a jail, never tell him what you are going to do with him.

865

'Let a thousand criminals go unpunished, no innocent man should be punished'— This is a cliche-ridden expression. No criminal should go unpunished and if one goes so, it shows the failure of the system. Acquittals are indicative of miscarriage of justice.

866

Inspite of the crimes they commit, the criminals live till they die.

867

In these days, you must go to a prison to find a criminal ? That was a nineteenth century concept. Now, people say that one should not go to jails to see criminals, for, many criminals—worth the name and status — live outside the prisons.

868

People have fear of the prisons until they go and stay there once. Once a person goes to jail, it means that he is branded as an ex-inmate of the prison. The social stigma continues till he dies. Once or many times in jails—that is not important for people who had been to the jails.

869

After all jails are constructed for human dwellings and the prison staff are also human beings. What is there, after all, in going to a jail for a short term stay ? It is an experience and many people do not get it. Some convicts take a light attitude to their incarceration.

870

Prisons have arrangements to provide food, shelter and clothing to the inmates. They are the basic requirements and many people living outside the prisons do not enjoy them. Some inmates like to be in jails so long as they are looked after. There are jail-birds also and they consider imprisonment as a blessing to live in an insured atmosphere of food, shelter and clothings.

871

Imprisonment has lost its relevance today; yet the society retains it as a punishment. This is so because, the society does not have an alternative to substitute imprisonment. See the helplessness in this regard!

872

Denial of freedom, denial of sex life, denial of family life, denial of social intercourse, denial of human pleasures etc. are there in imprisonment. The sufferers of these denials are the inmates in prisons, as well as their dependents. The real victims of imprisonment are living outside the prisons without food, shelter and clothings which are guaranteed to the inmates of prisons.

873

Once a prisoner is released, then he is put under surveillance in certain cases. In the pretext of offering security and in the name of conducting surveillance, there take place harassment, badgering or "hounding" of ex-prisoners by the law and order machinery. This is bad and can not be justified.

874

Prisons were constructed with an aim to punish the guilty. From the punitive philosophy, it came to peno-correctional and now to correctional philosophies. Yet, the prisons have miserably failed to achieve the aim of correction and rehabilitation. In the absence of an alternate arrangement, the society can not abolish the system now. Penologists are of view that the swing is ultimately towards abolishing of imprisonment as punishment. But, it will take time !

875

Jails in India were constructed with a punitive mind and in that way, everything is punitive in jails. Correction is now accepted as the objective of imprisonment and towards this end, some patchworks are done on the structural and functional areas in the prisons. The result has been that imprisonment is neither punitive nor correctional in its contents and approaches. This causes more harm than good for the rehabilitation of prisoners.

876

Prison staff, prison-buildings, prison rules and prison atmosphere are as old as the prisons themselves. What type of correction can come from such a deplorable state of affairs ? — ask the penologists everywhere in the Country.

877

The 'fallen brethren', 'the convicted offender', 'the criminal

VISITING JAILS TO SEE CRIMINALS?

IF YOU WANT TO SEE A CRIMINAL, LOOK AT THE MIRROR. THEN GO TO A JAIL AND SEE THE DIFFERENCE BETWEEN YOU AND THE CONVICTS.

after all' live at the mercy of the custodial staff who are concerned more with the custody than with the correction of the inmates. If correction is properly carried out, custody will not cause any head-ache to the prison staff.

878

The first Central Prison was constructed at Agra in 1846. More than one and half a century is now over. Penologists have now become sceptic about the effectiveness of imprisonment for the correction of crime-doers. As a result, open prisons, probation, parole, after care services etc. have come into being. These new introductions and innovations are yielding better results.

879

No police officer, no prosecutor, no judicial officer, no prison official, no criminologist may affirm that imprisonment is a success in reforming crime-doers. Penitentiary is a failure—that has been proved. Yet, it is being retained. Why?

880

Indian prisons are overcrowded by people who are detained under judicial custody. They make nearly 70 per cent of the prison population today. Is it not better to convert, prisons to detention centres rather than 'correctional centres'? A crime-doer needs correction only when he is convicted and experience shows that there takes place no correction worth its name in the existing prisons. As it is, why cann't we convert prisons to centres for detention and not for punishment?

881

Just go through the reports of the prison reform committees appointed from time to time in India from January 2, 1836. All these committees speak of corruption, laxity of discipline, uselessness of prison labour, overcrowding, lack of sanitary facilities, dearth of correctional influence, poor food and accomodation etc. The question is: Why should we retain such institutions at all—and that too for correcting the fallen citizens? Rediculous indeed!

882

Correction of a crime-doer can not come out from a purely punitive setting as it exists today in the prisons—and surely, the prisons can not reform anybody. If somebody does not become a recidivist, it is because he is influenced by corrective forces which are outside the prison atmosphere—says an ex-inmate from a central prison.

883

Punishment has corrective value only if the person to be corrected admits that the punishment is given with a motive to correct him. Punishment is only one method of correction.

884

If one goes by the records maintained in Indian prisons, there may not be a single instance of corporal punishment having been inflicted on an inmate for misconduct. The inmates, when interviewed, say that corporal punishments do have an important place in the maintenance of prison discipline. Who is right and who is wrong here?

885

A crime may be one man's act and several men's food. Convicts in prisons are the bread winners for the prison staff.

886

Prison is a unisex world. Naturally and necessarily, such a world will have its own abnormalities. Logically it follows that the abnormalities inherent in such a world will be a natural by-product. What to do to solve the inherent abnormalities?

887

A smile is a curve which can set a lot of things straight—This is a wise saying. Do the prison staff smile?—Do the inmates smile? If they do not, how can we straighten things in prison life?

888

Custody oriented prisons and correction oriented prisons—the first type is seen in reality and the second type in text books.

More over the custody-treatment quarrel is not yet over in Indian Penology. The new Prison Rules which may be passed by the Parliament also is biased in favour of custody more than correction?

889

Indian prisons are gradually and reluctantly becoming correctional centres and some prisons have indifferently adopted treatment programmes as well. Once a crime is committed, the treatment starts after several years. Usually, it takes three to four years for the system to complete investigation, prosecution, trial proceedings and to give a verdict of incarceration. If the crime-doer can adjust in society without committing another crime till the judgement is pronounced, there is no need for any treatment programmes for him at that belated time. Incarceration has only punitive value for such convicts.

890

Studies conducted on women prisoners in women's jails show that they were unhappy to lead a life in a one-sex society. Bitchiness of fellow prisoners was found to be intolerable. Most of them were engaged in malicious gossips. What is the therapeutic or treatment atmosphere in such an institution wherein women live a sort of abnormal life?

891

People or better 'the convicts after all' are not going to prisons voluntarily for treatment. They are forcibly brought there and the way they are taken to, received by and dealt with may show that they are sent to the prisons for the purpose of penalizing. Reality being so, they show resentment to any treatment programmes which, according to many, are ritualistic in every sense.

892

"Custodial officers order and the inmates obey"—this is the style of administration in Indian jails. The administration is autocratic. There is only blind obedience and no questions back. In such an atmosphere, what kind of treatment is possible ?

THE 'I' IN CRIMES

THERE IS NO CRIME WITHOUT AN 'I'. IF THE 'I' IS O.K., THEN EVERYTHING IS O.K. TAKE A MAGNIFYING GLASS AND LOOK AT THE CRIME. THEN YOU WILL SEE THE 'I'. THERE YOU ARE !

893

Custody, supervision and treatment—these are the three aspects of prison management today. Can treatment be effectively given in a custodial set up wherein the inmate is treated as a convict (without names, but only with numbers) by majority of the prison staff? As it is, the number of correctional staff is just a few and they enjoy a lesser status in prison management. What can they do to the inmates if at all they want to do something? They can do something if the custodial staff so permit them. What a deplorable condition indeed to see that the treatment modalities can not be independently fixed by the correctional staff!

894

The general public in India feel that the convicts are sent to prison as a punishment and not for correction. Correction of the prisoner is an idea known only to the criminologists, penologists and a few of the jail administrators. People do not see a change in the attitude of authorities towards the crime-doers although they speak a lot about correction and rehabilitation.

895

When does the correction start? No one is clear about it. Some say that it should start from the moment a crime-doer is arrested and should continue throughout the investigation, prosecution, trial, incarceration and even afterwards. What is happening today? The inmates say that they would like to see that their human rights are protected if at all their correction is not desired.

896

Custodial violence, custodial rape, custody-deaths, violation of human rights, violation of fundamental rights, violation of statutory rights, concoction of evidence, production of false-witnesses, manipulation of records and ultimately correction of the inmates! If all these things happen during the various stages of justice administration, then correction should be ensured more to the official agencies than to the so named crime-doers.

897

If innocent people are convicted, (some research studies

show that a fixed percentage of the inmates will be innocent people) or people are convicted on the production of false witnesses etc., then correction is needed more to the official agencies than to the inmates in correctional institutions. The inmates know more than anybody else how matters went against them and how they came to the prisons. All these affect their attitude towards correction in the prisons.

898

A punishment system based on fine, imprisonment or both does not contemplate institutional correction for those who are able to pay the fine and get out. Does it contemplate correction of a poor man who goes to jail because he is unable to pay the fine? The question is : "For whom does the system contemplate correction?

899

The penal philosophy during 1860 when the Indian Penal Code was enacted was punitive in content and approach. Punitive philosophy is changed into corrective only recently, but the Penal Code does not take into account the change in approaches. The Prison Rules too did not take into account the changed attitude. The result has been that the entire system of justice administration makes incarceration as punitive in letter and spirit. The system is called "criminal justice system" even now and justice to the criminal never meant correction of the crime-doer. In such a system, is there any scope for the correction of the crime-doer?

900

The penal laws of the Country still say that the offender "shall be punished with fine, imprisonment or both". When the laws speak of "punishment", they mean punishment—nothing more, nothing less. Penologists may say that, the concept of 'correction' should be brought in the statutes and the Indian Penal Code should be renamed as the Indian Correctional Code.

901

If correction is what is desired in justice administration, let us change all the words which have penal taste and connotations in the statutes. If correction is not what is intended, let us make everything punitive. There is no meaning in saying punitive correction in prison atmosphere. Prisons should be either penal or correctional. There is nothing called peno-correctional approach to crime-doers.

902

One and a half century year old penal laws, almost same old evidence laws, quarter of a century old procedural laws, a century old prison Act and we manage matters with very old concepts about justice administration. Criminal justice system paved the way to victim justice system which in turn paved the way to equal justice system. Equal justice system ensures justice to the crime-doers and to the victims of the offence. It is a balanced system.

903

Many or all jails have been constructed with an aim to inflict punishments. All the rules guiding prison management were drafted to see that prison-discipline is maintained and nothing more. Seeing that the treatment of prisoners is far away from being satisfactory, the United Nations brought out Standard Minimum Rules For the Treatment of Prisoners about four decades ago. Yet, some of the rules are not implemented and some with reluctance and objection and some others with indifference and cynicism. What to speak about correction then?

904

'New wine in old bottles'—it is almost like this that the correctional philosophy is being brought into prison management. New wine should be in new bottles, otherwise people may think that it is old wine kept so in old bottles. Any new idea implemented without sincerity of purpose can not and does not yield good results. People can not be fooled for long by preaching of correction and by practising of retributive-deterrent punishments. Some inmates are retributively dealt with even for minor misconducts—the intention being to cause deterrence among other inmates incase they too indulge in doing the same thing at a future date.

SIAMESE TWINS ? NO ?

ONE AND THE SAME PERSON IS THE CRIMINAL AND THE LAW ABIDING CITIZEN

ONE AND THE SAME MAN HAS CRIMINAL AND NON-CRIMINAL TRAITS

THERE IS A CRIMINAL IN EVERYMAN
AND
HE MAY HAVE A PLEASANT OR CRUEL FACE.
EVERYMAN IS MULTIFACED. HENCE LOOK INTO.
THYSELF TO SEE THE REAL CRIMINAL.

905

Correction of an individual or correction of the conditions causing criminality? Criminologists may advocate to have correction of the individual and of the social conditions etiologically responsible for causing crime and delinquency.

906

Correcting the society and the criminals is a social responsibility. The police, court, jail etc. have limited role to play in this regard. Obtain public support and society's cooperation to achieve the noble aims.

907

Family, school, religious organisations, community, social organisations, voluntary agencies, libraries, books, media etc. have a positive role to play towards crime control and correction of the crime-doers. Accept their role and appreciate their services.

908

Overcrowded prisons, inhuman treatment, unhygienic atmosphere, prolonged detention of undertrial prisoners, deterrent approaches, obnoxious staff-inmate contacts, abhorring living conditions, lack of treatment programmes and allegations of retributive, barbarous and inhuman approaches of the prison staff have repeatedly and very strongly attracted the attention of critics over the years. But what use?

909

The Indian Prison Act was essentially based on deterrent principles and the framers can not be blamed for doing so, because the correctional approach was not known to them. The Prison Act was more concerned with prison discipline and custodial management of the prisoners. The framers of the Act were not informed of the modern concepts of management and treatment of the inmates and therefore, they could not be blamed for what they did. The Prison Act gave more emphasis to prison offences and punishment to offenders and the framers were ignorant about the after effects of such an erroneous approach. A new Prison Act is going to come and the first reading of the draft Bill gives an impression that the framers are still moved by punitive philosophy more than correctional concepts.

910

Some estimates show that the prison population works out to be only 0.02 per cent of the total population in the Country (prison population (Dec. 1993) 1,96,240 and (Dec. 1992) 1,98,987). The prison population is indeed very small. Criminologists and penologists firmly believe that the prisoners (as they are only a few in number) can be easily managed in the most acceptable manner provided there is a will to do so. What is now seen is that a good many in prison administration are not serious about what they say.

911

People talk a lot about the police and their doings. People talk something about the courts in an audible or not audible manner. They do not talk anything much about the prisons and prisoners. They are treated as condemned souls who require nothing but contempt. People's attention should be made to focus on the issues of the fallen citizens into the mercy of State care and protection.

912

Prison administrators and policy makers are inclined to think that the prisons should have human miseries and inconvenience. They think that people may flow to the prisons if more facilities are provided in the jails. It shows how poorly educated they are on people's behaviour. They need more information about the dynamics of criminal behaviour and behaviour-modification techniques.

913

Studies conducted on prison administration show that there are many kinds of deviations among the prison staff and administrators. They are (1) disregard of the provisions contained in Jail Manuals and of the Prison Act, (2) showing blind eye and deaf ear to the latest techniques of correction and rehabilitation, (3) use of excessive force, violence and torture on prisoners who are helplessly living in a walled atmosphere, (4) involving in all sorts of corrupt practices, (5) and finally speaking aloud of many things they do not actually do or implement for the correction/rehabilitation of the prisoners.

914

Custodial violence and torture are quite common in prisons. Most unfortunately, the quantum, magnitude, intensity and extent of the inhuman treatment and torture in closed—maximum security—institutions can never be measured.

915

Many of the atrocities committed on the prisoners violate the jail Code, Penal Code and the human Code. But rarely one may hear of such atrocities committed on the inmates. The prisons are closed world and many things happening in such a world will also be closed to the public.

916

The psyche of the prison staff, prison administrators, inmates and so on must be transformed to effect change in the situation. Is this possible? It is possible only if there is a will to implement the decisions. The source of transformation lies with all of them and also with the governments holding power and purse to effect alterations.

CHAPTER - 9

CRIME AND COMMUNITY : IS REFORMATION OF A CRIME-DOER ACHIEVABLE?

917

The 'Enforcement Criminals' are those persons in law enforcement who violate laws for the purpose of enforcing laws. Use of third degree methods, concoction of evidence, manipulation of records etc. are examples in point since they are committed by people who are to execute laws. They are not considered as violations of laws. If they are not violations, then what are they?

918

'Enforcement Crimes' are informal arrests, illegal detentions, use of coercion during interrogation, employment of third degree methods etc. Though informal arrest is nothing but abduction, illegal detention is nothing but wrongful confinement, the personnel working in law enforcement do not consider their acts to be violations of law. Why?

919

Theft, burglary, murder, rape etc. are crimes *mala en se.* Criminologists do not ask whether they are "really" crimes as the actors are "really" criminals. They are condemned behavioural deviations. But, what about the 'Enforcement Crimes". They are also condemned behavioural deviations, yet people do not resent against openly as they are powerless to voice against the Enforcement Machinery.

920

An offence will be said to be an "ENFORCEMENT OFFENCE" in so far as it represents violation of the laws

❖ MARRIAGE ❖

FORCES WHICH MAKE A MAN TO MARRY A WOMAN ARE THE SAME-WHICH MAKE A WOMAN TO MARRY A MAN.

Man marries a woman and not an animal. He shares his life with her.

Woman has all the qualities and traits which man has and she commits all the crimes which man can.

Behind every crime, there may be a female voice and it may be provoking, encouraging, submitting, passively submitting, co-operating, contributing, instigating or soliciting etc.

FACTORS WHICH CAUSE MAN TO COMMIT CRIMES CAUSE WOMAN AS WELL TO COMMIT CRIMES.

constructed to govern law enforcement—in so far as the law violation takes place as part of the conduct of official works by the personnel engaged. By this, violation of human rights of a detainee is an enforcement offence.

921

Law Commissions, Police Commissions, Courts of law, Research Scholars and Criminologists have repeatedly made observations about 'Enforcement Criminality and Enforcement Criminals'. Recurrent reports in the media concerning enforcement criminality and unethical conducts have stimulated interest in enforcement crimes. Yet, the law enforcement officers seem to think that the 'Enforcement Crimes' are the necessary evils to enforce law. What a misfortune indeed!

922

"Let the crime-doer beware"—has always been dominant in the relationship between the enforcement officers and the crime-doers. The crime-doer thus becomes fully aware that 'enforcement criminality' is sure to come to him incase he is not 'co-operative' with the law enforcement officers. And 'co-operation' means 'co-operation' as defined by the law enforcement officers and not by the crime-doer.

923

The 'enforcement criminals' come from a group of people who are relatively comfortable. As a rule, most of them are psychopaths who have little or no guilt feeling for the crimes they commit.

924

The enforcement criminality is studied through association with criminals who have similar tendencies. Learning is the process by which the enforcement criminality is studied.

925

'Enforcement criminality' is committed for many things and one of the purposes is to make illicit income through the job. Some people call it 'corruption' while others call it 'bribery'. There are people who call it 'service money' etc.

926

Violence may be seen in 'Enforcement criminality'—e.g. use of third degree on a suspect—and the purpose may be to cause physical and mental damage to the direct victims handled by the enforcement agencies. It has also psychological effect produced on all members of the society. There is fear in the people.

927

In 'enforcement criminality', the enforcement officers, in a way, enforce recognition and subjectively feel important. They use not only violence but also terror to achieve recognition and achievement.

928

Every enforcement officer has a self-image, ego-ideal, self-respect and sense of oneself as an effectively functioning officer' commanding respect and attention from others. Whenever, the enforcement officer feels that he lacks his self-image or self-respect etc., he may resort to 'enforcement criminality' to establish himself as one having recognition and attention from others.

929

In democracy, people are very much against 'enforcement criminality'—particularly to the use of violence or terror. Excessive use of force, violation of human rights, death in custody, custodial violence including rape etc. are resented against by the people.

930

'Enforcement criminality' is tolerated by large segment of the society, for, the people think that it is necessary to maintain peace in society. There is a section of people who admit that the enforcement officers should terrorize the people to see that they maintain peace in society. There is yet another section of the people who say that terrorizing people should not be resorted to in a democracy.

931

In 'enforcement criminality', the enforcement officers define people's acts as criminal because they violate the criminal laws of the country or are interpreted by them as violating the criminal laws of the country. The same acts committed by the law-enforcement officers are not considered by them as violative of the criminal laws. They attach a lot of legal immunity to their otherwise criminal acts.

932

In 'enforcement criminality', a criminal act is defined as non-criminal because it is in the interest of the enforcement class to so define it.

933

In 'enforcement criminality', the members of the enforcement community will be able to violate the laws with immunity whereas the members of the subject class can not.

934

'Enforcement criminality' varies from department to department depending upon the areas in which each department can commit the same with immunity—total or partial.

935

The laws can not be enforced without enforcement agencies. The enforcement agencies can dirty the laws with their dirty tactics and it is these dirty tactics by which the laws are enforced are said to be containing in "enforcement criminality".

936

'Enforcement criminality' is justified by some saying that it is done for the larger interest of the society. There are several crimes committed by people for the larger interest of the society—but are treated as crimes by the enforcement officers. If that is so, there should not be any double standards in approaching one and the same issue in different ways.

937

On 'enforcement criminality', there was a judgement of the Allahabad High Court. In that judgement, the court observed that there was no organised criminals in the whole country whose record of crime would come anyway near to the same committed by that organised group which is called the Indian police. The

Criminal tendencies are seen both in the police and in the people.

Handcuffing a person without justifiable cause is a human right violation.

There is a policeman in every criminal and a criminal in every policeman.

Supreme Court of India, on appeal, further stated that there was a lot of truth behind that exaggerated virsion. Anyway, the judgements show the extent of 'enforcement criminality in police department.

938

'Enforcement criminality' and its extent are not known to the public as they are not reported. People are afraid to report enforcement criminality as they are not capable to suffer the consequences of such reportings. The media and pressure-groups etc. may be able to bring out enforcement criminality to the attention of the public.

939

A good many victims of enforcement criminality suffer the crimes committed on them. In a way this attitude is an encouragement to some of the enforcement criminals to freely indulge in their activities.

940

Eliciting information, coercing a confession, obtaining the continued presence, extracting money and favours, showing favouritism and partiality, concoing evidence, manipulating records, suppressing facts, suggesting false-hood, causing harassment, victimizing people, terrorizing the public, using third-degree methods—and so to say, any method by which the laws are violated by the people who are to enforce the law may be put under the term 'enforcement criminality'. They commit them during the course of their professional work.

941

Injustice caused to the people by enforcement criminality may be more than the justice done to the public by the enforcement agencies. For "justice through injustice" is the driving principle in enforcement criminality.

942

Some aspects of organised crimes—some aspects of white collar crimes—some aspects of blue collar crimes—some aspects of traditional crimes—when combined may result in "enforcement crimes."

943

The people who commit enforcement crimes are people who enforce the laws. Enforcing the law on enforcement officers for observance of the laws is indeed very difficult, if not impossible.

944

"Enforcement pathology" may be the underlying cause for enforcement criminality. Most of the enforcement officers who indulge in enforcement criminality are found to be enforcement psychopaths and moral morons.

945

What are the crimes you commit to enforce the laws?—The answer to this question may give the extent of enforcement criminality in that particular department.

946

"Ignorance of law is no excuse"—this principle in jurisprudence is known to all enforcement officers. Yet, they commit enforcement crimes' with immunity for the crimes they commit. What an injustice indeed?

947

The enforcement officers are on an advantageous position. They need to find out a behaviour and interpret it to be criminal in nature. The victim of their intepretation becomes the sufferer thereafter. Hence those who indulge in enforcement criminality are privileged ones.

948

Allegations are heard that false cases are registered against innocent people. Later, the courts of law acquit the accused finding that the case is a false one. At present, there is no law which says that this sort of enforcement criminality should be dealt with by providing compensation to the victims of enforcement criminality.

949

The police are legally bound to prevent crimes, investigate crimes, apprehend criminals, control criminality etc in a lawful manner. Often, they become the object of criticism. They are called brutal, corrupt and lawless. True or false the criticism may be, it shows the extent and intensity of enforcement criminality.

950

Down through the ages, the policeman's fertile imagination has designed and devised a variety of methods for committing enforcement crimes for enforcing law or in the pretext of enforcing law. Such methods may be for causing (1) financial loss, (2) physical torture, (3) social disgrace or (4) removal (social or psychological isolation) from the group etc.

951

'Enforcement criminals' who commit crimes during the course of their professional work (i.e., during the enforcement of law) develop a philosophy in support of their criminal activities. They consider their criminal acts as necessary, inevitable and natural for the execution of their job and as such do not normally have guilt feelings.

952

An 'Enforcement criminal' makes law violation a routine work. It is his success in the job, prestige in the work and fame in the department.

953

An enforcement criminal identifies himself as a successful enforcement officer until he is caught as one who violates the law without justification.

954

Every enforcement criminal like all other criminals, has a philosophy. "Like any other philosophy, it is a body of beliefs that are acquired in a process of adjustment over a period of time, organised into a system of principles, hardened and crystallised in terms of experience and used to explain the world and its way"—says Tannenhaum.

955

Every enforcement criminal violates law, for, he desires recognition, acceptance, good name and reputations. When he excels in his work, he is accepted as a hero and then he forgets about his crimes.

956

Though enforcement criminals are very prevalent in all departments, a few of them only are caught, prosecuted and convicted by criminal courts. Why? The enforcement agencies are not willing to catch them unless pressures are exerted on them.

957

Though the laws are not biased in favour of the enforcement criminals, the enforcement officers including the top level administration are inclined to favour the enforcement criminals. Consequently, they go on committing crimes without being caught by any body.

958

Enforcement criminality can not long persist without the cooperation and connivance of many on the enforcing department.

959

There is an argument which says that the enforcement departments should be permitted to commit 'enforcement crimes' to ensure better enforcement of law. It is just impossible to suppress enforcement criminality and therefore permit them to indulge in such activities for the larger good of the society. There is strong protest against this school of thought.

960

Custody death, custodial violence, corruption etc. are the offsprings of the permissiveness in carrying on enforcement criminality by the people and administration. Human rights activists, courts of law and civic-minded people are against the use of enforcement criminality in society.

961

'Enforcement pathology' may be a reason for 'enforcement criminality'. The enforcement officers lack adequate control over their emotions and therefore they are moved more by their emotions rather than reason.

962

'Super-ego controls' on the 'enforcement mind' are lacking and the environments in which the officers work do not exert adequate 'super ego' controls over them so much so that their 'id' impulses find expression in the enforcement pathology leading to enforcement criminality.

963

Enforcement officers exerted controls over the crimes in society and they did not exert controls over their own criminality. The people could not exert control over the enforcement criminality. The failure/refusal to exert administrative control over enforcement criminality together with the inability/ helplessness of the general public to prevent it helped towards the development of enforcement criminality. Many of the enforcement officers are still unquestioned kings in their area and jurisdiction so much so that they continue to commit enforcement criminality in many ways.

964

'Law enforcement' is a device designed and originated by the powerful for violating law' for their advantage. Politicians, social higher ups, the affluents, the influential and so on make use of it and often misuse the powers of the law enforcement agencies for their advantage. This too is enforcement criminality.

965

Those who live by committing enforcement crimes can not and do not have a peaceful service. They do not usually retire on superannuation.

966

'Never find your delight in another's misfortune'—This is a wise saying. Law is what the interpretation is. One can interpret

PROTECTION OF HUMAN RIGHTS BY POLICE
POLICE
are like a banian tree which gives shade to all sorts of people from all walks of life
INDISCRIMINATELY
They protect the HUMAN RIGHTS of all people from all walks of life indiscriminately
YET......
At times, the POLICE violate HUMAN RIGHTS. WHY?
POLICEMEN TOO COMPLAIN THAT THEIR HUMAN RIGHTS ARE NOT RESPECTED BY PEOPLE INCLUDING THE HIGHER-UPS IN POLICE SERVICE. WHY?

it "this way or that way". Interpreting the law in a manner ensuring misfortune to a person may be an act of delight to a section of the bureaucracy. See how the law can be interpreted to the advantage of others.

967

Muscle power, money power and mind power—all these powers may rule the people. But in law enforcement? Enforcement criminality can be reduced if and only if mind power rules the people who enforce the law.

968

A lot of precautions, arrangements and interest are taken or made to retain the convicted in the prison. What is the purpose behind it? To protect the interest of the prisoner? —the interest of the prison staff? — or the interest of justice? — or all of them? There is confusion on this count.

969

What is the interest a law enforcement officer has when he investigates a crime? To punish the criminal? If so, for what? — for protection of society? — for retribution ? — for deterrence ? — for correction? — for incapaciation? — for expiation? — for atonement? — for achieving a name and fame as an efficient investigator? — or all of them?

970

What is the commitment a prosecutor has when he argues a case against the accused? Is it to establish his name as an efficient prosecutor or something else?

971

What is the special motive of a defence lawyer when he argues in favour of the accused to get an acquittal? Is it to have a lucrative private practice or to establish justice in society? Every defence lawyer considers his in put—just or unjust, fair or unfair—as an investment to make more lucrative practice in law.

972

What interest has the jail staff towards the convicts? What is their commitment? Are they doing social work in prisons?

Their main role is to keep the custody of the inmates and for it they may do anything. If some one escapes from the jail custody, disciplinary action may be initiated against the jail staff. On the other-hand, if no one is corrected or rehabilitated, there is no departmental action against them. They are more worried about their existence and survival than the correction and rehabilitation of the inmates. For many of them, correction is a noble ideal but custody is a necessary evil.

973

Between custody and correction, custody assumes more importance. Whatever correction is possible in the existing custodial set-up and that is what is desired. If there is no correction, it is O.K; but no custody, it is dangerous.

974

Custodial set-up is not a conductive environment to convert law-violating people to law-abiding citizens. Yet, penologists argue that it is. Yes, it is. Then, what is the strategy? If strategy is fine, then why there are a lot of recidivists? Nobody answers these questions, but all are trying to perfect the sytem. Good. Best wishes!

975

Is correction possible for a person who is handcuffed, locked up, remanded, bailed out, convicted, incarcerated, penalized and finally released. At what stage, does he find correction? Correction via incarceration? If it works well, it is fine. Good luck!

976

A good number of law enforcement officers think that they know everything about the law and procedure in law enforcement; but in actuality, they need a lot of information in the matter. Yet, they try to enforce law by trial and error methods causing injustice and miscarriage of justice. And they say that they are administering justice!

977

What is the remedy for the 'enforcement injustice?'. There

may not be any effective remedy or if at all there is, it is very expensive and many do not go for it.

978

Ignorance of people about the law and their legal rights is the greatest strength for the ignorant law enforcement officers to involve in enforcement criminality.

979

'Ignorance of law is no excuse' is a dictum applicable to the ordinary people, but is found to be an excuse for the law-enforcement officers. They manage somehow to cover up their ignorance and execute their decisions in an ignorant way. And the victims of enforcement-ignorance suffer and tolerate everything done against them.

980

'Man is basically bad, but he can be made good-not always, not in everything and not every time'—This is a thought in criminology. The theory is true with respect to enforcement officers too. They try to locate the bad people and to make them good. But, if they themselves are bad, then? There comes 'enforcement criminality.'

981

Justice should be done—no—it should appear to others that justice has been done—This is a dictim in jurisprudence. The dictum has originated as the people found that there was enforcement criminality from time immemorial—from the time justice has been administered to law violators.

982

Let a thousand criminals go unpunished, no innocent person should be punished—This maxim has emerged from the people's notion of enforcement criminality—i.e., the law enforcement does not guarantee justice to all innocent people.

983

If criminals escape law enforcement, it is an evidence of enforcement criminality. Enforcement officers can surely see that

Be a welder
and not a wedge
WELDING HUMAN RELATIONS IS A POLICE JOB.
DO IT GRACEFULLY IF YOU CAN.
FAMILY PROBLEMS ARE NOT POLICE PROBLEMS....
LEAVE THEM TO EXPERTS

real criminals escape law enforcement.

984

Enforcement criminals are not called criminals because the people know that they will commit enforcement criminality if they are called criminals. Registering of false cases is also put under enforcement criminality by criminologists today.

985

Being in law enforcement, officers are likely to develop a pro-prosecution attitude and may become punitive in their approaches. This attitude/approach decides the extent and intensity of enforcement criminality.

986

People in general do not have any favourable disposition to those who work in enforcement departments and it is primarily because the people think that the officers are susceptiable to influences/introductions/recommendations. Some people express their resentment and displeasure when they see that the officers are dispossessed of their power and authority. Susceptibility to influences/introductions/recommendations results in enforcement criminality.

987

Enforcement criminality is not confined to the police only. It is applicable to many other departments like the sale tax, forest, central excise and customs, P.W.D., water-authority, State excise etc. The victims of enforcement criminality can say better the extent and magnitude of enforcement crimes committed against them.

988

Enforcement officers lose their credibility in public when they commit enforcement crimes. Many a time, the victims of enforcement criminality may be ignorant of the crimes committed against them. The moment they come to know, it will be too late for them to do any thing for saving themselves from the evil effects of such crimes.

DELINQUENCY

READING TABLE AT HOME IS THE BREEDING PLACE FOR MANY VICES AMONG CHILDREN

CHILDREN READ FILTHY BOOKS

– TAKE TO SMOKING

– SMOKE GANJA

– CONSUME DRUGS

– ENJOY PHONOGRAPHY

– AND DO MANY MORE OF SIMILAR CRIMINAL ACTS WHEN THEY ARE ALONE IN THEIR ROOMS WHICH ARE NOT CARED BY PARENTS

KEEP A WATCH ON CHILDREN WHEN THEY ARE IN THE READING ROOM

989

'Enforcement criminality' is responsible for 'abortion of justice'. Abortion of justice means justice aborted for the safety of the crime doers or for the gain of the enforcement officers.

990

Bureaucratic injustice, enforcement criminality and abortion of justice are interconnected. Perhaps, one can not exist without the other. Enforcement criminality contains bureaucratic injustice and abortion of justice.

991

Bureaucrats—this is a status assigned to people when they assume some offices in Government. Their sense of justice and behavioural dynamics do not come all on a sudden—one day, too soon. Bureaucratic injustice has a history—a history of development and it starts from their homes—from their mothers—from their parents—from the family atmosphere. Hence, bureaucratic injustice begins at home.

992

No enforcement officer is an affected person—victim—in a crime. His interest is that he represents the State—i.e., the public which is a faceless mass. What is or will be his special interest to see that the crime-doer is punished? What is his special interest to see that the crime-doer is acquitted? His special interest will be decided by his values and considerations to which he is susceptible. If his value is that enforcement criminality is no criminality he continues to commit it; otherwise, he refrains from it. If he is vulnerable to introductions, influences or considerations he commits enforcement criminality according to the impact or effect of such influences, recommendations and influences. The question here is "What is justice" during enforcement?

993

What are the crooked ways the law is enforced? The answer to this question gives the extent and magnitude of enforcement criminality.

994

Familarity breeds contempt. Likewise, people who enforce

Vicarious Aggression

AGGRESSION MAY BE (1) Sadistic

(2) Masochistic

(3) Vicarious

Vicarious aggression means that the aggression has been directed to an object or person representing the person against whom one becomes aggressive.

ANTISOCIAL PERSONALITY—Diagnostic criteria

A. Current age atleast 18

B. Onset before age 15 as indicated by a history of three or more of the following before that age.

(1) truancy

(2) Expulsion or suspension from school for misbehaviour

(3) Delinquency arrest

(4) Running away from home overnight atleast twice while living in parental or parental surrogate home

(5) Persistent lying

(6) Repeated sexual intercourse in a casual relationship.

(7) Thefts

(8) Vandalism

(9) School grades markedly below expectations

(10) Chronic violation of rules at home and/or at school

(11) initiation of fights

(From D.S.M.III)

law need not necessarily show due respect to law and lawful procedures. They may violate law as an easy cut to enforce law and there comes the crime called enforcement criminality.

995

Enforcement criminality can be committed individually or collectively by the law enforcement officers. Often the explanation for the commission of enforcement criminality will be ununderstandable to people who are not enforcement officers. Every crime has etiological factors and all criminals justify their acts.

996

No one desists from committing a crime for want of reasons or justifications. Enforcement criminals are not an exception to this rule.

997

Every verdict of acquittal from a court of law shows the extent, variety and magnitude of enforcement criminality.

998

On an average it is found that 30 to 40 per cent of the newspapers in India gives news and views about crimes, criminals and criminality. Out of them, nearly half—a little more or a little less—may be about enforcement criminality. People who read the news helplessly make comments about enforcement criminality and their tolerate it. People's tolerating attitude, in a way, encourages enforcement criminality—say the criminologists.

999

What are the various departments which are empowered to enforce law? A rough estimate may show that the crimes committed by these departments may be more than the crimes committed by the people at a given time. For, the crimes committed by people are visible where as the same by the enforcement officers are not.

1000

'God of small things'—This may be the name of a book. In enforcement, many officers think that they are the gods of small mortals' and that is the reason why they commit enforcement crimes-feel the criminologists.

1001

'Little things' irritate the law enforcement officers in uniform more than what they do when they are not in uniform. The 'Uniform Ego' makes them to behave the way they do and it gives to them surcharged energies and makes them to behave in a perverted way. "Uniform Ego Feeling" is the cause of enforcement criminality.

1002

Law Enforcement Officers know the laws better than their victims. The ignorance of the victims is a reason for the commission of enforcement criminality and for this purpose the victims are sometimes pressured to sign on blank papers or to give undertakings on matters which they may not otherwise like to undertake. The law enforcement officers thus make their otherwise weaker positions to be stronger and more justifiable.

1003

There are many people who argue for the criminal, and their welfare. There are no one to plead for the law enforcement officers and to expose their difficulties in enforcing law—why? This is a question asked by many law enforcement officers. The answer to this question is simple. People see the extent and magnitude of enforcement criminality and they see that people are sinned against more than sinning and that is the reason why they are pleading for the criminals and for their welfare.

1004

Enforcing criminality, enforcement criminality and enforced criminality are the three varieties of crimes during the enforcement of law.

1005

Enforced for?— The answer to this question gives the extent and magnitude of enforcement criminality. The question is—enforced for justice or not? If it is not for justice, then it becomes an enforcement criminality.

1006

Crime is crime, criminals are criminals, criminal justice is criminal justice, victims are victims, enforcement is enforcement, courts are courts, prosecutions are prosecutions, trials are trials, convictions are convictions, acquittals are acquittals, deterrence is deterrence, reformation is reformation, correction is correction and thus the process moves on and so does the world.

Think—

DO WE ENSURE JUSTICE

TO THE CRIME-DOER? TO HIS FAMILY?

TO THE VICTIMS OF CRIME?

TO THE SOCIETY? TO HUMANITY? If not ensure it here and now.

BIBLIOGRAPHY

Alexander, G.W., (1957), *Jail Administration*, Springfield : Charles C.Thomas.

Alphonse L. Earayil and James Vadackumchery, (1985), *Police and the Society*, Thiruvananthapuram : Kairali.

Alphonse L. Earayil and James Vadackumchery, (1985), Public Relations at the Cutting Edge Level : Case Study Material, Delhi : National.

Asch, Sidney, H., (1968), *Police Authority and the Rights of the Individual*, New York : Arce.

Banton, Michael (1965), *The Policeman in the Community*, New York : Basic Books.

Berkley, G.E., (1969), *The Democratic Policemen*, Beston : Beacon Press.

Black, Algerner, D., (1968), The People and the Police, New York : McGraw Hills.

Carney, L.P. (1980) *Corrections : Treatment and Philosophy*, Englewood Cliffs; Prentice Hall.

Clemmer, D., (1958), *The Prison Community*, New York : Volt, Rinehart, and Winston.

Clift, Raymond, E., (1956), *A Guide to Modern Police Thinking*, Cincinnati : W.H. Anderson.

Coffey, Allen, R., (1975), *Correctional Administration*, Englewood Cliffs, Prentice Hall.

Fox, Vernon, (1973), *Introductions to Corrections*, Washington : Reston Publishing Company.

German, A.C., (1958), *Police Personnel Management*, Springfield : Charles C. Thomas.

Gourley, G.O., (1953), *The Police and the Public*, Springfield : Charles C. Thomas.

Grunhurt, Max, (1943), *Penal Reform*, Oxford : University Press.

Government of India, (1970), *Model Prison Manual*, Faridabad : GOIP.

Heinoke, J.M., (ed.), (1978) *Economic Models of Criminal Behaviour*, Amsterdem : North Holland.

Jonkins, Robert, (1970), *Keeping the Police*, New York : Harper and Row.

Johnson, E.M., (1964), *Crime, Correction and Society*, Homewood : Dorsey.

Kay, Barbara, A., and Clyde B. Vedder, (1963), *Probation and Parole*, Springfield : Charles C. Thomas.

Likert, R., (1961), *New Patterns of Management*, New York : Mc Graw Hills.

Lynch, Ronald, G., (1975), *The Police Manager*, Boston; Holbrook Press.

Morris, N., (1974), *The Future of Imprisonment*, Chicago : Chicago University Press.

Murton, T.O., (1976) *The Dilemma of Prison Reforms*, New York : Holt, Rinehart and Winston.

Newman, Charles L., (1970), *Concept of Treatment in Probation and Parole Supervision*, Probation and Parole, New York : John Wiley and Sons.

Portune, R.G., (1971) *Changing Adolescent Attitude Towards Police*, Cincinnati : Anderson.

Reckless, W.C., (1970), *The Crime Problem*, Bombay, Vakils, Feffer and Simons.

Ruchelman, L., (ed.), (1973), *Who Rules the Police ?*, New York : New York University Press.

Singh, M.K., (1984), *A Decade of Crime—A Sociological Analysis*, Indian Journal of Criminology, Madras : 12, 2.

Srivastava, S.P., (1987), *The Probation System : An Evaluative Study, Lucknow* : Print House.

Studt, Elliot, (1959), *Education For Social Workers in Correctional Field*, New York : Council of Social Work Education.

Tappan, P.W., (1960), *Crime, Justice and Correction*, New York : McGraw Hills.

United Nations (1955), *Proceedings of the First United Nation's Congress on the Prevention of Crime and Treatment of offenders*, New York : United Nations.

Vadackumchery James, (1997) *The Police, The People and Criminal Justice,* New Delhi : APH Publishing Corporation.

Vadackumchery James, (1997), *The Police, The Accused and Criminal Justice,* New Delhi : APH Publishing Corporation.

Vadackumchery James, (1997) *Indian Police and Miscarriage of Justice,* New Delhi : APH Publishing Corporation.

Vadackumchery James, (1997), *The Police, The Court and Injustice,* New Delhi : APH Publishing Corporation.

Vadackumchery James and John Kattakayam, (1995), *Human Behaviour and Law Enforcement,* New Delhi : Ashish Publishing House.

Vollmer, August (1936), *The Police and Modern Society,* Berkeley : University of California Press.

Wilbus Larre, (1939), *Parole with Honor,* Princeton : University Press.

Whitaker, Ben, (1964), *The Police,* Baltimore : Penguin Books.

Zeeman, E.C. (1974), *A Model For Prison Disturbances,* British Journal of Criminology, 17, 3.

Withus Laure, (1939) *People with Heroes.* Princeton : Princeton University Press.

INDEX